# Google Sheets Functions

A step-by-step guide

by

Barrie Roberts

# Table of Contents

**Introduction to functions** ............................................................................................. 6
   So, what are Google Sheet formulas? .................................................................... 6
   What are functions? ................................................................................................ 7

**1: AVERAGE, MAX, MIN** ............................................................................................ 8
   =AVERAGE() ............................................................................................................ 8
   =MIN() ..................................................................................................................... 10
   Automatic formulas ............................................................................................... 10

**2: COUNT and COUNTA** .......................................................................................... 11
   =COUNT() .............................................................................................................. 11
   =COUNTA() ............................................................................................................ 12

**3: IF** .......................................................................................................................... 17
   Example 1 - Has the student passed or failed? .................................................... 17
   Example 2 - Referring to a cell ............................................................................. 19
   Example 3 - Dealing with blank spaces and making your data look prettier ...... 20
   Example 4 - Nested IF functions and multiple options ....................................... 22
   Example 5 - Making decisions based on words not just numbers ...................... 24

**4: CONCATENATE (inc TEXT, CONCAT and &)** ....................................................... 26
   Example 1 - Joining two names together ............................................................ 26
   Example 2 - Making website URLS from information in different cells ............. 27
   Example 3 - Combining a range of cell values to make a complete part number ... 28
   Example 4 - Concatenating formulas .................................................................. 29
   Example 5 - Making sentences and adding dates in the current format ............ 29
   Example 6 - Creating addresses on different lines .............................................. 30
   Further notes ......................................................................................................... 31
   & - AND operator ................................................................................................... 32

**5: VLOOKUP (inc IFERROR and ARRAYFORMULA)** ................................................ 33
   Example 1 - Look up a book number and get the name of who has it .............. 33
   Example 2 - Display a message instead of an error, if something cannot be found ... 35
   Example 3 - Finding values within ranges ........................................................... 36
   Example 4 - Including formulas in a VLOOKUP function ................................... 37
   Example 5 - Using wildcards in VLOOKUP .......................................................... 38
   Example 6 - Looking up multiple values in a table ............................................. 39
   Example 7 - Retrieving multiple values from a table .......................................... 41
   Example 8 - Retrieving multiple values from a table (part 2) ............................. 42
   Example 9 - Using Named Ranges with VLOOKUP ............................................ 43

**6: OR & AND (inc WEEKDAY)** ................................................................................. 48
   Example 1 - How does the OR function work? And how does it work with IF? .. 48
   Example 2 - Checking to see if at least one race time is below the target time .. 49
   Example 3 - Looking at more than two race times ............................................. 49
   Example 4 - Using the AND function ................................................................... 50
   Example 5 - Using AND to check if the values are within a range ..................... 50
   Example 6 - Categorising the values based on certain conditions ..................... 51
   Example 7 - Using functions within an OR or AND function ............................. 52

**7: COUNTIF, SUMIF, COUNTIFS, SUMIFS** .............................................................. 54
   Example 1 - COUNTIF: Counting the number of instances of a specific number ... 54
   Example 2 - COUNTIF: Counting how many values are over a certain number .. 55
   Example 3 - COUNTIF: Counting the number of times a word or phrase appears in a range ... 56
   Example 4 - COUNTIF: Using a cell reference to find instances of whatever has been written in that cell ... 56

Example 5 - COUNTIF: Using wildcards to look for broader values ............................................. 57
Example 6 - COUNTIF: Counting dates ......................................................................................... 58
Example 7 - SUMIF: Adding up the number of products sold on a particular date ..................... 59
Example 8 - SUMIFS: To find the quantity sold within a date range ............................................ 60
Example 9 - COUNTIF: Counting how many students are above average ................................... 61
Example 10 - COUNTIFS: Highlighting duplicate rows ................................................................ 62

## 8: FILTER ............................................................................................................................. 66
Example 1 - Filtering a list by a piece of text ............................................................................... 66
Example 2 - Filtering a list by those who still need to pay .......................................................... 67
Example 3 - Filtering a table by a specific date ........................................................................... 68
Example 4 - Filtering a table between two dates ........................................................................ 69
Example 5 - Filtering a table by a specific month ....................................................................... 70
Example 6 - Counting the number of values that meet the filter condition ............................... 71
Example 7 - Summing up the total of values that meet the filter condition .............................. 72
Example 8 - Filtering a table using one criterion OR another ..................................................... 73

## 9: IMPORTRANGE ................................................................................................................ 75
Example 1 - How to use IMPORTRANGE ...................................................................................... 76
Example 2 - Open-ended ranges .................................................................................................. 78
Example 3 - Multiple IMPORTRANGES on the same sheet .......................................................... 79
Example 4 - Pre-formatting an imported range .......................................................................... 81

## 10: PROPER, UPPER, LOWER, TRIM ....................................................................................... 85
Example 1 - Using the PROPER function to capitalize each word ............................................... 85
Example 2 - Using the UPPER function to capitalize all letters ................................................... 86
Example 3 - Using the LOWER function to put words into lowercase ........................................ 86
Example 4 - Using the PROPER and TRIM functions to clean up text ......................................... 87
Example 5 - Using ARRAYFORMULA to copy PROPER function to all rows ................................. 87
Example 6 - Capitalizing only the first letter of a sentence and putting the rest in lowercase .. 88
Bonus Example - Changing a name to initials ............................................................................. 89

## 11 - TRANSPOSE .................................................................................................................. 91
Example 1 - Changing a single column or row of data ................................................................ 91
Example 2 - Converting 2 vertical columns to 2 horizontal ones ............................................... 91
Example 3 - Converting multiple horizontal rows into vertical columns ................................... 92

## 12: ISEMAIL, ISNUMBER, ISURL, NOT .................................................................................... 94
Example 1 - Checking email addresses ........................................................................................ 94
Example 2 - Checking for numbers .............................................................................................. 95
Example 3 - Checking website addresses (URLs) ......................................................................... 96
Example 4 - Displaying different text depending on whether it's TRUE or FALSE ...................... 96
Example 5 - Adding conditional formatting ................................................................................. 97
Example 6 - Using custom formula to add colour to cells with the data in it............................. 100
Example 7 - Using NOT in a custom formula to highlight what isn't true................................... 101

## 13: UNIQUE, COUNTUNIQUE, SORT ...................................................................................... 104
Example 1 - Using the UNIQUE function to list unique occurrences in a list.............................. 104
Example 2 - Using UNIQUE with SORT to sort the unique list .................................................... 105
Example 3 - Making a drop-down menu from a list ................................................................... 106
Example 4 - Making an alphabetical drop-down menu from a list ............................................ 107
Example 5 - Using COUNTUNIQUE to count how many things you have in the list, whilst ignoring duplicates ......... 108
Example 6 - Using UNIQUE to look for unique occurrences with 2 or more criteria ................. 108

## 14: NOW, TODAY, DAY, MONTH, YEAR, HOUR, MINUTE, SECOND......................................... 111
Example 1 - Getting the current date and time .......................................................................... 111
Example 2 - Getting today's date and using it in calculations .................................................... 112

Example 3 - Extracting the day from a date .................................................................................................. 113
Example 4 - Extracting the month or year / Find out how old someone is ................................................. 115

## 15: WEEKDAY, WORKDAY, NETWORKDAYS, EDATE, EOMONTH, CHOOSE .................................. 117
Example 1 - What day of the week was a particular date? ........................................................................ 117
Example 2 - Returning the day of the week as text not as a number ........................................................ 118
Example 3 - Find out the date a number of days from a given date ......................................................... 118
Example 4 - How many working days are there between two dates? ...................................................... 119
Example 5 - Easily adding start of the month and end of the month dates ............................................ 120
Example 6 - Working out the number of days in a month ........................................................................ 121
Example 7 - Working out the number of working days in a month ......................................................... 122

## 16: GOOGLETRANSLATE, DETECTLANGUAGE .................................................................................... 123
Example 1 - Translating from one language to another ........................................................................... 123
Example 2 - Detecting a language .............................................................................................................. 123
Example 3 - Detecting a language and translating it ................................................................................ 124
Example 4 - Automatically translating board vocabulary ........................................................................ 124
Example 5 - Having a conversation where neither person speaks the other's language ....................... 125

## 17: OFFSET .................................................................................................................................................. 127
Example 1 - Creating dynamic ranges to maintain an average formula ................................................. 127
Example 2 - Dynamically calculating the sales of the last X months ...................................................... 130

## 18: IMAGE ................................................................................................................................................... 132
Example 1 - Inserting an image from Drive ............................................................................................... 132
Example 2 - Inserting an image within a cell using the IMAGE function ................................................ 134

## 19: ROUND, ROUNDUP, ROUNDDOWN ................................................................................................. 137

## 20: HYPERLINK ......................................................................................................................................... 138
Example 1 – Renaming a hyperlink ............................................................................................................ 138
Example 2 – Linking to a Google Document ............................................................................................. 139
Example 3 – Linking to a particular sheet ................................................................................................. 139
Example 4 – Linking to a particular cell .................................................................................................... 140

## 21: INDEX and MATCH .............................................................................................................................. 142
Example 1 - Finding the classroom a specific teacher is in ...................................................................... 142
Example 2 - Finding who is in a particular classroom (looking up to the LEFT in a table) ..................... 143
Example 3 - The effect of inserting a column in a table on an INDEX/MATCH and a VLOOKUP formula .. 144
Example 4 - Returning more than one column of information ................................................................ 145
Example 5 - Matching a range and not an exact figure ............................................................................ 145

## 22: QUERY ................................................................................................................................................... 147
Analysing questionnaire feedback .............................................................................................................. 147
Example 1 - Selecting the relevant data from the master data ................................................................ 147
Example 2a - Filter by a teacher's name .................................................................................................... 148
Example 2b - Filter by a teacher's name using a cell reference ............................................................... 149
Example 2c - Filter by a teacher's name and sort the date in descending order .................................... 150
Example 3a - Filter the data between 2 dates ........................................................................................... 151
Example 3b - Filter between 2 dates using cell references ...................................................................... 152
Example 3c - Filter between 2 dates and by teacher ................................................................................ 153
Example 4 - Filter against various criteria ................................................................................................ 154
Example 5a - Returning the averages of data ........................................................................................... 155
Example 5b - Returning the averages of data and ordering them .......................................................... 156
Example 6 - Pivot information using QUERY not pivot tables ................................................................. 157
Analysing a HR database ............................................................................................................................ 157
Example 7 - Returning average salaries per department ........................................................................ 158
Example 8 - Listing salaries per employee in descending order ............................................................. 158

Example 9 - Limiting the number of results ........................................................................................... 159
  Example 10 - Ordering by more than 1 criteria ..................................................................................... 160
  Example 11 - Relabelling column headers.............................................................................................. 160

# *A note from the author* ............................................................................................. **162**

# *Index* ........................................................................................................................ **167**

© Barrie Roberts

# Introduction to functions

Cells may be the building blocks of a spreadsheet but functions and formulas are the power behind it. They are there to help you with the hard work of calculations and to avoid having to do things manually. Whether it's a simple addition formula or highly complicated logical and mathematical functions, there are hundreds of functions to choose from and these can be combined in almost unlimited ways. However, most users end up only using a select few repeatedly.

**So, what are Google Sheet formulas?**

Let's start with a simple example. Let's add up four numbers (1, 3, 2, 4), in this example the goals scored by 4 players in a game.

To add these up on the sheet, I type in **=1+3+2+4** and press Enter to get the result. The equals sign (=) is what tells the sheet that it's a formula and not just some text.

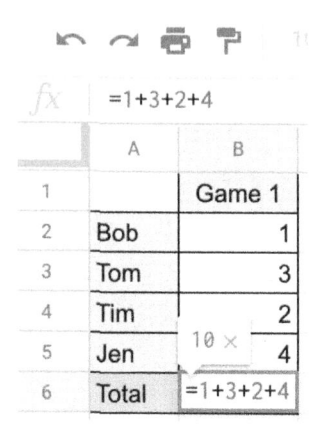

I can also do this by referring to the cells the numbers are in, i.e. **=B2+B3+B4+B5** then press Enter.

Clicking on B6, you can see the formula in the formula bar.
Now, imagine if I had 100 players, the formula would be pretty long to work out the total!
**=B2+B3+B4+.....+B101**
Well, this is where a function can help out.

## What are functions?

Functions are a collection of different keywords that will do specific jobs. Functions have a certain syntax that need to be used. They start with an equals sign (like formulas do) and then they have a pair of brackets. Inside the brackets is where you define what you want the function to do.

## =sum()

The one we want in this example is the sum function, as we want to sum up the goals scored. In cell B6 let's type in the sum function to sum up the total goals scored:

## =sum(B2:B5)

This is telling the sheet to sum up the range from B2 to B5 (i.e. the goals scored in game 1).

| | A | B |
|---|---|---|
| 1 | | Game 1 |
| 2 | Bob | 1 |
| 3 | Tom | 3 |
| 4 | Tim | 2 |
| 5 | Jen | 4 |
| 6 | Total | =sum(B2:B5) |

| | A | B |
|---|---|---|
| 1 | | Game 1 |
| 2 | Bob | 1 |
| 3 | Tom | 3 |
| 4 | Tim | 2 |
| 5 | Jen | 4 |
| 6 | Total | 10 |

If I had 100 players, the function would be the same size and something like this:

## =sum(B2:B101)

Much better than typing in 100 cell references!

So, the idea of this book is to show you how to use some of the most useful functions in Google Sheets. It starts with the basic ones like SUM, which we've just seen and takes you through to more advanced areas like VLOOKUP, IMPORTRANGE, and QUERY.

I feel the best way to learn these is by following examples and in every chapter, I will take you through several examples showing you different aspects of the function and various uses of it.

The examples start with the basic syntax of the function and build up to more complex formulas, but I explain each step along the way. So, don't worry, these are much easier than maybe you think!

# 1: AVERAGE, MAX, MIN

Now we know how to write a function, let's look at some more common ones.

In this example, we'll look at analysing some exam results. I've already entered in the students' exam results and now I want to know the average mark, the highest and the lowest mark.

|    | A | B |
|----|---|---|
| 1  | EXAM RESULTS | |
| 2  | Name | Marks |
| 3  | Fred | 76% |
| 4  | Barney | 56% |
| 5  | Wilma | 87% |
| 6  | Betty | 71% |
| 7  | Roxanne | 91% |
| 8  | Ed | 72% |
| 9  | Mercedes | 57% |
| 10 | Scott | 66% |
| 11 | Mark | 89% |
| 12 | Natasha | 85% |
| 13 | Average: | |
| 14 | Highest: | |
| 15 | Lowest: | |

## =AVERAGE()

Underneath the exam results, I'm going to add the average mark.

In cell B13, type in **=average(B3:B12)** and press Enter

This gets the range from B3 to B12 and works out the average mark (the mean). This is much quicker and simpler than adding up all the marks individually and then dividing by the total number of students (i.e. (B3+B4+....+B11+B12)/10)

| | A | B |
|---|---|---|
| 1 | **EXAM RESULTS** | |
| 2 | **Name** | **Marks** |
| 3 | Fred | 76% |
| 4 | Barney | 56% |
| 5 | Wilma | 87% |
| 6 | Betty | 71% |
| 7 | Roxanne | 91% |
| 8 | Ed | 72% |
| 9 | Mercedes | 57% |
| 10 | Scott | 66% |
| 11 | Mark | 89% |
| 12 | Natasha | 85% |
| 13 | Average: | =AVERAGE(B3:B12) |
| 14 | Highest: | |
| 15 | Lowest: | |

| | A | B |
|---|---|---|
| 1 | **EXAM RESULTS** | |
| 2 | **Name** | **Marks** |
| 3 | Fred | 76% |
| 4 | Barney | 56% |
| 5 | Wilma | 87% |
| 6 | Betty | 71% |
| 7 | Roxanne | 91% |
| 8 | Ed | 72% |
| 9 | Mercedes | 57% |
| 10 | Scott | 66% |
| 11 | Mark | 89% |
| 12 | Natasha | 85% |
| 13 | Average: | 75% |
| 14 | Highest: | |
| 15 | Lowest: | |

# =MAX()

Now, let's find the highest mark.

In cell B14 type in **=max(B3:B12)** and press Enter.

| | A | B |
|---|---|---|
| 1 | **EXAM RESULTS** | |
| 2 | **Name** | **Marks** |
| 3 | Fred | 76% |
| 4 | Barney | 56% |
| 5 | Wilma | 87% |
| 6 | Betty | 71% |
| 7 | Roxanne | 91% |
| 8 | Ed | 72% |
| 9 | Mercedes | 57% |
| 10 | Scott | 66% |
| 11 | Mark | 89% |
| 12 | Natasha | 85% |
| 13 | Average: | 75% |
| 14 | Highest: | =MAX(B3:B13) |
| 15 | Lowest: | |

| | A | B |
|---|---|---|
| 1 | **EXAM RESULTS** | |
| 2 | **Name** | **Marks** |
| 3 | Fred | 76% |
| 4 | Barney | 56% |
| 5 | Wilma | 87% |
| 6 | Betty | 71% |
| 7 | Roxanne | 91% |
| 8 | Ed | 72% |
| 9 | Mercedes | 57% |
| 10 | Scott | 66% |
| 11 | Mark | 89% |
| 12 | Natasha | 85% |
| 13 | Average: | 75% |
| 14 | Highest: | 91% |
| 15 | Lowest: | |

## =MIN()

And let's find the lowest mark.

In cell B15 type in **=min(B3:B12)** and press Enter.

| | A | B |   | | A | B |
|---|---|---|---|---|---|---|
| 1 | EXAM RESULTS | | | 1 | EXAM RESULTS | |
| 2 | Name | Marks | | 2 | Name | Marks |
| 3 | Fred | 76% | | 3 | Fred | 76% |
| 4 | Barney | 56% | | 4 | Barney | 56% |
| 5 | Wilma | 87% | | 5 | Wilma | 87% |
| 6 | Betty | 71% | | 6 | Betty | 71% |
| 7 | Roxanne | 91% | | 7 | Roxanne | 91% |
| 8 | Ed | 72% | | 8 | Ed | 72% |
| 9 | Mercedes | 57% | | 9 | Mercedes | 57% |
| 10 | Scott | 66% | | 10 | Scott | 66% |
| 11 | Mark | 89% | | 11 | Mark | 89% |
| 12 | Natasha | 85% | | 12 | Natasha | 85% |
| 13 | Average: | 75% | | 13 | Average: | 75% |
| 14 | Highest: | 56% × % | | 14 | Highest: | 91% |
| 15 | Lowest: | =MIN(B3:B12) | | 15 | Lowest: | 56% |

Great! With three simple functions, we now have a good idea of how well the class is doing.

**Automatic formulas**

When you typed the equals sign, you might have noticed, that Sheets gave you a formula suggestion. In this case, this was the one we wanted and we can save time typing out the formula, and just press Enter to add the formula to the cell.

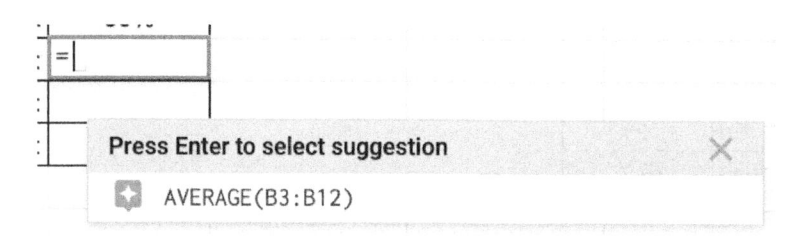

Press Enter to select suggestion

AVERAGE(B3:B12)

# 2: COUNT and COUNTA

In this chapter, we're going to look at COUNT and COUNTA. COUNT counts the number of numbers there are in a range and COUNTA counts the number of cells in a range with text in them.

In this example, I want to work out the percentage of students that sat an exam.

This has three parts to it, and will introduce you to not only two more functions but to how functions can work together to give you the information you need.

## =COUNT()

So, what I need to work out is:

***The number of students who sat the exam*** divided by ***the total number of students***, and display that number as a percentage

|    | A | B |
|----|---|---|
| 1  | **Name** | **Marks** |
| 2  | Fred | 76% |
| 3  | Barney | Not present |
| 4  | Wilma | 87% |
| 5  | Betty | Not present |
| 6  | Roxanne | 57% |
| 7  | Ed | 72% |
| 8  | Mercedes | 91% |
| 9  | Scott | 66% |
| 10 | Mark | Not present |
| 11 | Natasha | 85% |
| 12 | No of exams sat: | |
| 13 | No of students: | |
| 14 | % students sitting exam: | |

First, let's find out how many students sat the exam.

In B12, type in **=COUNT (B2:B11)** and as always press Enter

The **COUNT** function, adds up all the **numbers** in the range selected. It ignores the text "not present". So, here 7 students sat the exam.

| | A | B |
|---|---|---|
| 1 | **Name** | **Marks** |
| 2 | Fred | 76% |
| 3 | Barney | Not present |
| 4 | Wilma | 87% |
| 5 | Betty | Not present |
| 6 | Roxanne | 57% |
| 7 | Ed | 72% |
| 8 | Mercedes | 91% |
| 9 | Scott | 66% |
| 10 | Mark | Not present |
| 11 | Natasha | 85% |
| 12 | No of exams sat: | =COUNT(B2:B11) |
| 13 | No of students: | |
| 14 | % students sitting exam: | |

| | A | B |
|---|---|---|
| 1 | **Name** | **Marks** |
| 2 | Fred | 76% |
| 3 | Barney | Not present |
| 4 | Wilma | 87% |
| 5 | Betty | Not present |
| 6 | Roxanne | 57% |
| 7 | Ed | 72% |
| 8 | Mercedes | 91% |
| 9 | Scott | 66% |
| 10 | Mark | Not present |
| 11 | Natasha | 85% |
| 12 | No of exams sat: | 7 |
| 13 | No of students: | |
| 14 | % students sitting exam: | |

# =COUNTA()

Next, let's add up the total number of students.

In B13, type in **=COUNTA(A2:A11)** and press Enter

This time, the **COUNTA** function adds up all cells which <u>aren't blank</u>, in the range selected. It doesn't matter what type of data is in the cells. So, it's correctly worked out that they are 10 students because there are 10 names in that range.

| | A | B |
|---|---|---|
| 1 | **Name** | **Marks** |
| 2 | Fred | 76% |
| 3 | Barney | Not present |
| 4 | Wilma | 87% |
| 5 | Betty | Not present |
| 6 | Roxanne | 57% |
| 7 | Ed | 72% |
| 8 | Mercedes | 91% |
| 9 | Scott | 66% |
| 10 | Mark | Not present |
| 11 | Natasha | 85% |
| 12 | No of exams sat: | 7 |
| 13 | No of students: | =COUNTA(A2:A11) |
| 14 | % students sitting exam: | |

| | A | B |
|---|---|---|
| 1 | **Name** | **Marks** |
| 2 | Fred | 76% |
| 3 | Barney | Not present |
| 4 | Wilma | 87% |
| 5 | Betty | Not present |
| 6 | Roxanne | 57% |
| 7 | Ed | 72% |
| 8 | Mercedes | 91% |
| 9 | Scott | 66% |
| 10 | Mark | Not present |
| 11 | Natasha | 85% |
| 12 | No of exams sat: | 7 |
| 13 | No of students: | 10 |
| 14 | % students sitting exam: | |

Finally, I want to know the percentage of students who sat the exam, so I need to divide the number sat into the total, i.e. cell B12 divided by B13.

In B14, type in **=B12/B13** and press Enter.

| | A | B |
|---|---|---|
| 1 | **Name** | **Marks** |
| 2 | Fred | 76% |
| 3 | Barney | Not present |
| 4 | Wilma | 87% |
| 5 | Betty | Not present |
| 6 | Roxanne | 57% |
| 7 | Ed | 72% |
| 8 | Mercedes | 91% |
| 9 | Scott | 66% |
| 10 | Mark | Not present |
| 11 | Natasha | 85% |
| 12 | No of exams sat: | 7 |
| 13 | No of students: | 0.7 × 10 |
| 14 | % students sitting exam: | =B12/B13 |

|   | A | B |
|---|---|---|
| 1 | **Name** | **Marks** |
| 2 | Fred | 76% |
| 3 | Barney | Not present |
| 4 | Wilma | 87% |
| 5 | Betty | Not present |
| 6 | Roxanne | 57% |
| 7 | Ed | 72% |
| 8 | Mercedes | 91% |
| 9 | Scott | 66% |
| 10 | Mark | Not present |
| 11 | Natasha | 85% |
| 12 | No of exams sat: | 7 |
| 13 | No of students: | 10 |
| 14 | % students sitting exam: | 0.7 |

To turn the number in cell B14 into a percentage, click on B14 then click on the percentage (%) button on the toolbar.

£   %   .0

|   | A | B |
|---|---|---|
| 1 | **Name** | **Marks** |
| 2 | Fred | 76% |
| 3 | Barney | Not present |
| 4 | Wilma | 87% |
| 5 | Betty | Not present |
| 6 | Roxanne | 57% |
| 7 | Ed | 72% |
| 8 | Mercedes | 91% |
| 9 | Scott | 66% |
| 10 | Mark | Not present |
| 11 | Natasha | 85% |
| 12 | No of exams sat: | 7 |
| 13 | No of students: | 10 |
| 14 | % students sitting exam: | 70.00% |

If you feel comfortable with the above, you could have quickened the process by putting the function, that you entered into B12 and the one into B13, together and this would give you the same result. Note, you only enter the equals sign at the start of the formula.

## =COUNT(B2:B11)/COUNTA(A2:A11)

All of the functions above (except **COUNTA**) can also be quickly accessed via the menu shortcut toolbar, by clicking on the sigma button and a drop-down menu appears with the 5 most common ones, plus access to the rest underneath.

Σ ▾

- SUM
- AVERAGE
- COUNT
- MAX
- MIN

This starts you off with the function and all you need to do is add the cells or range it needs to use.

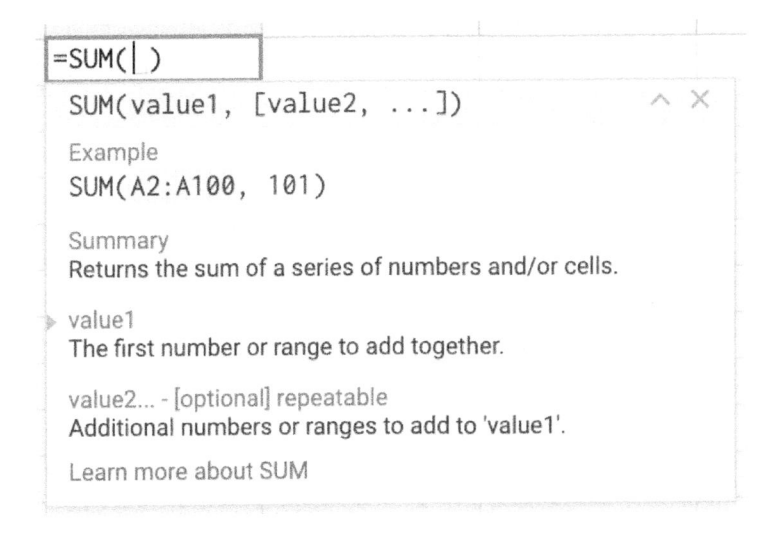

```
=SUM( )
SUM(value1, [value2, ...])
Example
SUM(A2:A100, 101)

Summary
Returns the sum of a series of numbers and/or cells.

value1
The first number or range to add together.

value2... - [optional] repeatable
Additional numbers or ranges to add to 'value1'.

Learn more about SUM
```

Notice that when you start typing a function or use the shortcut above, Sheets provides you with some help.

In the first row, it's telling you what kind of data it expects in the function.

The second row, gives you an example of how to fill it out.

The third row tells you what the function does.

The final rows, give you more information on the data you need to include within the brackets.

All of this is extremely useful, especially when using a function for the first time or indeed when you can't quite remember what data it needs inside it.

You may have also noticed that while you write out the function or formula, a little "speech bubble" appears telling you the result of your formula so far. It's a great way to check your formula is producing the result you're expecting, as you're writing it.

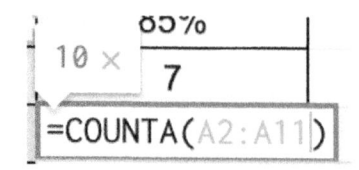

```
10 × 85%
      7
=COUNTA(A2:A11)
```

# 3: IF

Sometimes you're not sure what's going to be on your sheet and in your cells, and you want to show a value or piece of text, depending on what's in those cells. This is where the IF function comes in.

It's like what we use in English, IF this happens, I'll do this, IF NOT I'll do something different. It's one of the functions I use all the time, and I'm sure you will!

**Example 1 - Has the student passed or failed?**

Here, I have 4 students who have done an exam and I want to show who has passed or failed. The pass mark is 60% and clearly with just 4 students this is easy to see, but imagine a sheet with for example, 100 students.

|   | A | B | C |
|---|---|---|---|
| 1 | **Exam marks** | | |
| 2 | Student | Exam mark | Pass or fail? |
| 3 | John | 65% | |
| 4 | George | 59% | |
| 5 | Ringo | 62% | |
| 6 | Paul | 48% | |
| 7 | Pass mark = 60% | | |

In cell C3, start off with by typing **=IF(**

Here, the help box will appear. In the first line, it's showing you what it needs you to fill out.

|   | A | B | C | D | E |
|---|---|---|---|---|---|
| 1 | **Exam marks** | | | | |
| 2 | Student | Exam mark | Pass or fail? | | |
| 3 | John | 65% | =IF( | | |
| 4 | George | 59% | | | |
| 5 | Ringo | 62% | | | |
| 6 | Paul | 48% | | | |
| 7 | Pass mark = 60% | | | | |

IF(logical_expression, value_if_true, value_if_false)

Example
IF(A2 = "foo", "A2 is foo", "A2 is not foo")

Summary
Returns one value if a logical expression is 'TRUE' and another if it is 'FALSE'.

logical_expression
An expression or reference to a cell containing an expression that represents some logical value, i.e. 'TRUE' or 'FALSE'.

value_if_true
The value that the function returns if 'logical_expression' is 'TRUE'.

value_if_false
The value that the function returns if 'logical_expression' is 'FALSE'.

Learn more about IF

There are 3 parts:

"logical expression" - This just means what are you trying to test for. It needs to be a true or false question. For example, in this case, Is the exam mark more than or equal to 60%?

"value_if_true" - This is what you want to put in the cell, if the answer to your question is TRUE, i.e. the exam mark IS more than or equal to 60%.

"value_if_false" - This is what you want to put in the cell, if the answer to your question is FALSE, i.e. the exam mark IS NOT more than or equal to 60% (in other words, less than).

So, to continue with our function, next we write the question we want answering, the logical expression. We want to know if the exam mark in cell B3 is more than 60%. First, we add the cell reference B3.

|   | A | B | C | D |
|---|---|---|---|---|
| 1 | **Exam marks** | | | |
| 2 | Student | Exam mark | Pass or fail? | |
| 3 | John | 65% | =IF(B3 | |
| 4 | George | 59% | IF(logical_expression, value_if_false) | |
| 5 | Ringo | 62% | | |
| 6 | Paul | 48% | Example IF(A2 = "foo", "A2 is foo") | |
| 7 | Pass mark = 60% | | | |

Then we add 'the more than' symbol and the equals sign, which together mean 'more than or equal to', then we add the number, in this case 0.6 (note, this is not 60, as 60% = 0.6).

`=IF(B3>=0.6`

Then we need to tell it, what to do if the above question is TRUE or FALSE. I want it to add the word "PASS" if it's true and "FAIL" if it's not. Add a comma, then in double quotes write PASS and FAIL as below. Then close the bracket. So, your function should now look like this:

`=IF(B3>=0.6,"PASS","FAIL")`

Note, as we type the formula, we get the speech bubble telling us the result of it, i.e. it will show PASS in the cell.

```
PASS
or fail?
=IF(B3>=0.6,"PASS","FAIL")
```

Press Enter and as you can see in cell C3, the word PASS has been displayed, as John has indeed got more than 60% in his exam.

Click on cell C3 and drag the little blue square down to copy the function down to the other cells. Straight away we can see George and Paul haven't passed the exam.

|   | A | B | C |
|---|---|---|---|
| 1 | **Exam marks** | | |
| 2 | Student | Exam mark | Pass or fail? |
| 3 | John | 65% | PASS |
| 4 | George | 59% | FAIL |
| 5 | Ringo | 62% | PASS |
| 6 | Paul | 48% | FAIL |
| 7 | Pass mark = 60% | | |

## Example 2 - Referring to a cell

What happens if the teacher believes the exam was too hard and the pass mark should now be 50%? In the example above, we would have to go back into the function and change the 0.6 to 0.5. Possible but more work for us. We can avoid that by referring to a cell where the pass mark has been written in.

Here the pass mark is in cell B7.

|   | A | B | C |
|---|---|---|---|
| 1 | **Exam marks** | | |
| 2 | Student | Exam mark | Pass or fail? |
| 3 | John | 65% | PASS |
| 4 | George | 59% | PASS |
| 5 | Ringo | 62% | PASS |
| 6 | Paul | 48% | FAIL |
| 7 | Pass mark: | 50% | |

Here's the original formula:

```
=IF(B3>=0.6,"PASS","FAIL")
```

Let's change the 0.6 to the cell reference, B15. Note, I've had to put the dollar signs in, as this makes it an absolute reference, i.e. it will always refer to that cell, even when I copy the formula down the rows to the other students.

```
=if(B3>=$B$7,"PASS","FAIL")
```

I copy it down the rows as before and it changes George's result to a PASS.

|   | A | B | C |
|---|---|---|---|
| 1 | **Exam marks** | | |
| 2 | Student | Exam mark | Pass or fail? |
| 3 | John | 65% | PASS |
| 4 | George | 59% | PASS |
| 5 | Ringo | 62% | PASS |
| 6 | Paul | 48% | FAIL |
| 7 | Pass mark: 50% | | |

Now, by changing the pass mark in cell B7, this will automatically update the Pass/Fail results in the table. For example, changing it to 70%, automatically shows that all the students would have failed.

|   | A | B | C |
|---|---|---|---|
| 1 | **Exam marks** | | |
| 2 | Student | Exam mark | Pass or fail? |
| 3 | John | 65% | FAIL |
| 4 | George | 59% | FAIL |
| 5 | Ringo | 62% | FAIL |
| 6 | Paul | 48% | FAIL |
| 7 | Pass mark: 70% | | |

So, certainly use references if you may change the formula values in the future.

### Example 3 - Dealing with blank spaces and making your data look prettier

With the examples so far, before adding the exam marks, the table would look like the one below, i.e. in the pass/fail column it's stating that they have failed because the Exam mark cells are blank.

|   | A | B | C |
|---|---|---|---|
| 1 | **Exam marks** | | |
| 2 | Student | Exam mark | Pass or fail? |
| 3 | John | | FAIL |
| 4 | George | | FAIL |
| 5 | Ringo | | FAIL |
| 6 | Paul | | FAIL |
| 7 | Pass mark: 60% | | |

To get around this, there is a really good use of the IF function, which only shows the content in the cells, if another cell has something in it.

We need to add a check at the start of our formula, so see if the cell has an exam mark in it. If it's blank then we want it to make the pass/fail column blank.

The start of the formula is as below. It looks in cell B3 and if it IS blank (two double quotes with nothing in between means nothing), then we add nothing (again two double quotes).

`=IF(B3="", "",`

So, this is if the check is TRUE, now we end with the original formula, as this will run if the cell ISN'T blank (i.e. the false result). Then we end it all with a second closed bracket, as follows:

`=IF(B3="", "", IF(B3>=$B$7,"PASS","FAIL"))`

So, just to summarise that, the first part checks to see if B3 is empty, if it is it makes C3 empty. If it isn't it checks to see what has been added in B3 is more than or equal to 60%, if it is it writes PASS, if not it writes FAIL in C3.

Here's what the table looks like now. Nice and tidy waiting for results to be added.

|   | A | B | C |
|---|---|---|---|
| 1 | **Exam marks** | | |
| 2 | Student | Exam mark | Pass or fail? |
| 3 | John | | |
| 4 | George | | FAIL |
| 5 | Ringo | | FAIL |
| 6 | Paul | | FAIL |
| 7 | Pass mark: 60% | | |

|   | A | B | C |
|---|---|---|---|
| 1 | **Exam marks** | | |
| 2 | Student | Exam mark | Pass or fail? |
| 3 | John | | |
| 4 | George | | |
| 5 | Ringo | | |
| 6 | Paul | | |
| 7 | Pass mark: 60% | | |

As soon as we do, the function starts working out if the exam mark is pass or fail.

|   | A | B | C |
|---|---|---|---|
| 1 | **Exam marks** | | |
| 2 | Student | Exam mark | Pass or fail? |
| 3 | John | 65% | PASS |
| 4 | George | 59% | FAIL |
| 5 | Ringo | | |
| 6 | Paul | | |
| 7 | Pass mark: 60% | | |

**Example 4 - Nested IF functions and multiple options**

In the example above, we used two IF functions together. This is called nesting and this can be extremely powerful and allow you to check the multiple situations, not just the basic, is one thing true or false. The above example provided us with 3 possible outcomes:

1) Cell B3 was blank -> Make C3 blank

2) Cell B3 wasn't blank -> Was C3 more than or equal to 60%? -> Yes, so write "PASS"

3) Cell B3 wasn't blank -> Was C3 more than or equal to 60%? -> No, so write "FAIL"

In this example, let's look at a company where they offer different discount rates to their customers, depending on the quantity they buy. Here's the table summarising the discounts:

|   | A | B |
|---|---|---|
| 1 | **Discount rates** | |
| 2 | Quantity | Discount |
| 3 | 1-99 | 2% |
| 4 | 100-499 | 5% |
| 5 | 500-999 | 7% |
| 6 | 1000+ | 10% |

So, up to 99 products you get a 2% discount, up to 499 you get a 5% discount, and so on.

So, we want to create a formula which will check if they have bought 1000 or more, if so, apply the 10% discount, if not check if they have bought 500 or more, if so, apply the 7 % discount, etc.

We're going to add the formulas in the Discount column, initially in D11.

|    | Customers | Quantity bought | Price | Discount | Total |
|----|-----------|-----------------|-------|----------|-------|
| 10 |           |                 |       |          |       |
| 11 | Widgets LTD | 600 | $100.00 | | |
| 12 | Thingamajigs PLC | 250 | $100.00 | | |
| 13 | Wotdayamacalits | 20 | $100.00 | | |
| 14 | GizmosRUs | 2000 | $100.00 | | |
| 15 | StuffnMoreStuff | 999 | $100.00 | | |

First, we check for the largest quantity: Is the quantity in cell B11 more than or equal to 1000, if it is, then put the 10% discount from cell B6.

=if(B11>=1000,$B$6,

Second, we check for next discount. If the quantity in B11 is more than or equal to 500, if so, put the 7% discount from B5.

=if(B11>=1000,$B$6, if(B11>=500, $B$5,

Note, that in the first test we checked if it was 1000 or more, then IF NOT, then check to see if is 500 or more.

We continue until we get to the last possibility, which is, is it 1 or more.

=if(B11>=1000,$B$6, if(B11>=500, $B$5, if(B11>=100, $B$4,

If it isn't, then it must be 0 (assuming no mistakes or typos), so we end the formula with a 0, to show we would offer a discount if they didn't buy anything!

`=if(B11>=1000,$B$6, if(B11>=500, $B$5, if(B11>=100, $B$4, if(B11>=1, $B$3, 0))))`

Even though they can look complicated and sometimes be quite long, a nested IF statement always follows the same pattern:

IF(check a condition, action if TRUE, if FALSE check a condition, action if TRUE, if FALSE check a condition....until the last one...action if TRUE, action if everything is FALSE)

So, in our example, we have a customer, the quantity they bought, the price of the product. Then the discount which will be applied based on the quantity they bought, using the formula above, and finally the cost with the discount (quantity x price-discount).

Here Widgets Ltd, have a 7% discount as they bought more than 500 but less than 1000.

|    | Customers   | Quantity bought | Price    | Discount | Total       |
|----|-------------|-----------------|----------|----------|-------------|
| 11 | Widgets LTD | 600             | $100.00  | 7%       | $55,800.00  |

As before, we copy the formula down the rows and we can see the different discounts that have been applied immediately.

|    | Customers         | Quantity bought | Price    | Discount | Total        |
|----|-------------------|-----------------|----------|----------|--------------|
| 11 | Widgets LTD       | 600             | $100.00  | 7%       | $55,800.00   |
| 12 | Thingamajigs PLC  | 250             | $100.00  | 5%       | $23,750.00   |
| 13 | Wotdayamacalits   | 20              | $100.00  | 2%       | $1,960.00    |
| 14 | GizmosRUs         | 2000            | $100.00  | 10%      | $180,000.00  |
| 15 | StuffnMoreStuff   | 999             | $100.00  | 7%       | $92,907.00   |

**Example 5 - Making decisions based on words not just numbers**

So far, we've looked at whether a figure is larger than another, but we can also set an IF function to do something if it matches a piece of text.

Here we have the same customers, but this time the company's decided to offer certain customers an extra discount. In column J, they've written YES or NO to determine who gets the extra discount.

| | A | B | C | D | E | F | G |
|---|---|---|---|---|---|---|---|
| 1 | Customers | Quantity bought | Price | Discount | Total | Extra Discount 5% | Final Total |
| 2 | Widgets LTD | 600 | $100.00 | 7% | $55,800.00 | NO | |
| 3 | Thingamajigs PLC | 250 | $100.00 | 5% | $23,750.00 | YES | |
| 4 | Wotdayamacalits | 20 | $100.00 | 2% | $1,960.00 | NO | |
| 5 | GizmosRUs | 2000 | $100.00 | 10% | $180,000.00 | YES | |
| 6 | StuffnMoreStuff | 999 | $100.00 | 7% | $92,907.00 | NO | |

Here I want an IF statement that will add the extra discount to the total if it states "YES" in column F or to leave the total the same as it is in column I.

So, for the first customer, I write the following formula:

`=if(F2="YES", E2*0.95,E2)`

This checks to see if F2 is YES, and if it does, it gets the total and multiplies it by 0.95 (to work out a 5% discount), and if it doesn't, then it just gets the original total from E2.

Below we can see that the extra discounts have been applied to the rows with a YES.

| | A | B | C | D | E | F | G |
|---|---|---|---|---|---|---|---|
| 1 | Customers | Quantity bought | Price | Discount | Total | Extra Discount 5% | Final Total |
| 2 | Widgets LTD | 600 | $100.00 | 7% | $55,800.00 | NO | $55,800.00 |
| 3 | Thingamajigs PLC | 250 | $100.00 | 5% | $23,750.00 | YES | $22,562.50 |
| 4 | Wotdayamacalits | 20 | $100.00 | 2% | $1,960.00 | NO | $1,960.00 |
| 5 | GizmosRUs | 2000 | $100.00 | 10% | $180,000.00 | YES | $171,000.00 |
| 6 | StuffnMoreStuff | 999 | $100.00 | 7% | $92,907.00 | NO | $92,907.00 |

The IF function is very powerful and can automate so many things, just as long as you create a condition (or question) that can be answered TRUE or FALSE. It will then use just pure logic to give you the answer.

When checking for various values such as in example 4, the IF formulas can get quite long, in these cases it would be better to use something like VLOOKUP, which looks up the value in the table, but that's in a future chapter. For now, enjoy trying out the IF function.

# 4: CONCATENATE (inc TEXT, CONCAT and &)

Concatenation. What on earth does that mean? Put simply, this is putting different pieces together to create a whole. We can have values in different cells and use the CONCATENATE function to join them together to create one combined piece. Here I'll go through some examples of how to use this function, building up from the very basics to more sophisticated ways to use it, combing it with other functions. So, let's dive straight in.

**Example 1 - Joining two names together**

In this first example, we have some names which from our system have been stored in separate cells. One column for their first name and one for their surname. What we want to do is combine the two to create their full name and store it in column C.

|   | A | B | C |
|---|---|---|---|
| 1 | **First name** | **Surname** | **FULL NAME** |
| 2 | Fred | Flintstone |   |
| 3 | Wilma | Flintstone |   |
| 4 | Barney | Rubble |   |
| 5 | Betty | Rubble |   |

In cell C2, we write a CONCATENATE function to join the contents of column A and B. As we write the function, we can see that the function needs some strings (text, numbers, etc) to put together.

|   | A | B | C | D | E |
|---|---|---|---|---|---|
| 1 | **First name** | **Surname** | **FULL NAME** |   |   |
| 2 | Fred | Flintstone | =CONCATENATE( |   |   |
| 3 | Wilma | Flintstone | CONCATENATE(string1, [string2, ...]) |   |   |
| 4 | Barney | Rubble | Example CONCATENATE("hello", "goodbye") |   |   |
| 5 | Betty | Rubble | Summary Appends strings to one another. |   |   |
| 6 |   |   |   |   |   |
| 7 |   |   | string1 The initial string. |   |   |
| 8 |   |   |   |   |   |
| 9 |   |   | string2... - [optional] repeatable More strings to append in sequence. |   |   |
| 10 |   |   | Learn more about CONCATENATE |   |   |

In the brackets, we refer to cell A2 (Fred), add a comma, then refer to cell B2 (Flintstone).

```
=CONCATENATE(A2,B2)
```

As you can see it's added the two names together, the only problem is, is that there's no space between the two.

|   | A | B | C |
|---|---|---|---|
| 1 | **First name** | **Surname** | **FULL NAME** |
| 2 | Fred | Flintstone | FredFlintstone |

To remedy this, we need to add a space in between the cells A2 and B2 in the formula, like this:

=CONCATENATE(A2," ",B2)

Now we have the words with a space in the middle.

|   | A | B | C |
|---|---|---|---|
| 1 | **First name** | **Surname** | **FULL NAME** |
| 2 | Fred | Flintstone | Fred Flintstone |

Once we've written the formula for one cell, we can drag it down to the rows below to fill the table.

|   | A | B | C |
|---|---|---|---|
| 1 | **First name** | **Surname** | **FULL NAME** |
| 2 | Fred | Flintstone | Fred Flintstone |
| 3 | Wilma | Flintstone | Wilma Flintstone |
| 4 | Barney | Rubble | Barney Rubble |
| 5 | Betty | Rubble | Betty Rubble |

**Example 2 - Making website URLS from information in different cells**

We can use the same principle to create individual URLs. Here we have a table where we have the main website address and the various pages on it. On the right, we're going to join them together.

|   | A | B | C |
|---|---|---|---|
| 1 | Home | Sub page | URL |
| 2 | www.widgets.com/ | gadgets |  |
| 3 | www.widgets.com/ | thingamajigs |  |
| 4 | www.widgets.com/ | wotsits |  |

This time instead of add the individual cell references, we can write a range in between the brackets:

`=CONCATENATE(A2:B2)`

This creates the specific page links which we can now share and use.

|   | A | B | C |
|---|---|---|---|
| 1 | Home | Sub page | URL |
| 2 | www.widgets.com/ | gadgets | www.widgets.com/gadgets |
| 3 | www.widgets.com/ | thingamajigs | www.widgets.com/thingamajigs |
| 4 | www.widgets.com/ | wotsits | www.widgets.com/wotsits |

**Example 3 - Combining a range of cell values to make a complete part number**

We can continue the idea of using a range of values to create, for example, here a part number. The part number is made up of a location, parent type, subset and the part and are combined to create an individual part number.

|   | A | B | C | D | E |
|---|---|---|---|---|---|
| 1 | Location | Parent Type | Subset | Part | Full Part Number |
| 2 | 001 | 123 | 345245 | 3434200 |  |
| 3 | 001 | 123 | 234544 | 3434201 |  |
| 4 | 002 | 123 | 454252 | 3434202 |  |
| 5 | 003 | 456 | 245345 | 3434203 |  |

If we just want to combine all the numbers together, we can just refer to the range where the values are:

`=CONCATENATE(A2:D2)`

|   | A | B | C | D | E |
|---|---|---|---|---|---|
| 1 | Location | Parent Type | Subset | Part | Full Part Number |
| 2 | 001 | 123 | 345245 | 3434200 | 11233452453434200 |
| 3 | 001 | 123 | 234544 | 3434201 | 11232345443434201 |
| 4 | 002 | 123 | 454252 | 3434202 | 21234542523434202 |
| 5 | 003 | 456 | 245345 | 3434203 | 34562453453434203 |

As the number is long and a little difficult to read, we may want to add some dashes to identify the individual parts of the number. Like the spaces we added above, we just add the dashes in between the cell references:

`=CONCATENATE(A2, "-", B2, "-", C2, "-", D2)`

|   | A | B | C | D | E |
|---|---|---|---|---|---|
| 1 | Location | Parent Type | Subset | Part | Full Part Number |
| 2 | 001 | 123 | 345245 | 3434200 | 1-123-345245-3434200 |
| 3 | 001 | 123 | 234544 | 3434201 | 1-123-234544-3434201 |
| 4 | 002 | 123 | 454252 | 3434202 | 2-123-454252-3434202 |
| 5 | 003 | 456 | 245345 | 3434203 | 3-456-245345-3434203 |

**Example 4 - Concatenating formulas**

Here we want to show on a website the quantity of each product we have, and also the total of all the things we have. In cell C6, we write the following formula:

`=CONCATENATE(SUM(A2:A5), " ", "Things")`

First, we are summing the contents of column A (the quantities), we add a space, then add the word "Things".

|   | A | B | C |
|---|---|---|---|
| 1 | Quantity | Product | No of Products |
| 2 | 23 | widgets | 23 widgets |
| 3 | 12 | gadgets | 12 gadgets |
| 4 | 123 | thingamajigs | 123 thingamajigs |
| 5 | 2 | wotsits | 2 wotsits |
| 6 |   |   | 160 Things |

**Example 5 - Making sentences and adding dates in the current format**

Here we'd like to show today's date as part of a complete sentence.

|   | A | B | C |
|---|---|---|---|
| 1 | 26/05/2019 |   | Today's date is 26/05/2019 |

To do this, we first write the text we want (the fixed part of the sentence), in this example, "Today's date is " (notice the space at the end). Then we need to get the date which is in cell A1. If we just write A1, then the date won't appear in a date format, rather it will appear as a number, like this:

| | A | B | C |
|---|---|---|---|
| 1 | 26/05/2019 | | Today's date is 43611 |

So, we need to adjust the formula, so that it gets the text in A1 and puts it into a date format using the TEXT function:

`=CONCATENATE("Today's date is ",TEXT(A1,"DD/MM/YYYY"))`

The TEXT function gets the contents of the cell and displays it using the format in the second part of the function, i.e. DD/MM/YYYY.

Today's date is 26/05/2019

**Example 6 - Creating addresses on different lines**

Here we want to create some addresses but we want each cell to appear on its own line, ready to be printed. These are UK style addresses and we have the street number and name, the town, county and then the post code.

| | A | B | C | D | E |
|---|---|---|---|---|---|
| 1 | Street | Town | County | Post Code | Full address |
| 2 | 23, Mayfield Road | Netherend | Gwent | NP14 1AB | |
| 3 | 55, Birchwood St | Taymouth | Devon | TA10 4XY | |
| 4 | 432, Beaumont Ave | Brizington | Avon | BR5 4TW | |

To add a line break after each line of the address, we need to use the character number 10: **char (10)**. We add a cell reference, then add the char(10) after each one.

`=CONCATENATE(A2,char(10),B2,char(10),C2,char(10),D2)`

This puts the full addresses in column E, with each part of the address on a different line.

|   | A | B | C | D | E |
|---|---|---|---|---|---|
| 1 | **Street** | **Town** | **County** | **Post Code** | **Full address** |
| 2 | 23, Mayfield Road | Netherend | Gwent | NP14 1AB | 23, Mayfield Road<br>Netherend<br>Gwent<br>NP14 1AB |
| 3 | 55, Birchwood St | Taymouth | Devon | TA10 4XY | 55, Birchwood St<br>Taymouth<br>Devon<br>TA10 4XY |
| 4 | 432, Beaumont Ave | Brizington | Avon | BR5 4TW | 432, Beaumont Ave<br>Brizington<br>Avon<br>BR5 4TW |

**Further notes**

**CONCAT v CONCATENATE**

If you've typed out a CONCATENATE function, you may have noticed that there's another one called CONCAT. This works in a similar way...so what's the difference?

Basically, in Sheets CONCAT is only used to combine two values, whereas there is no limit with CONCATENATE (within reason).

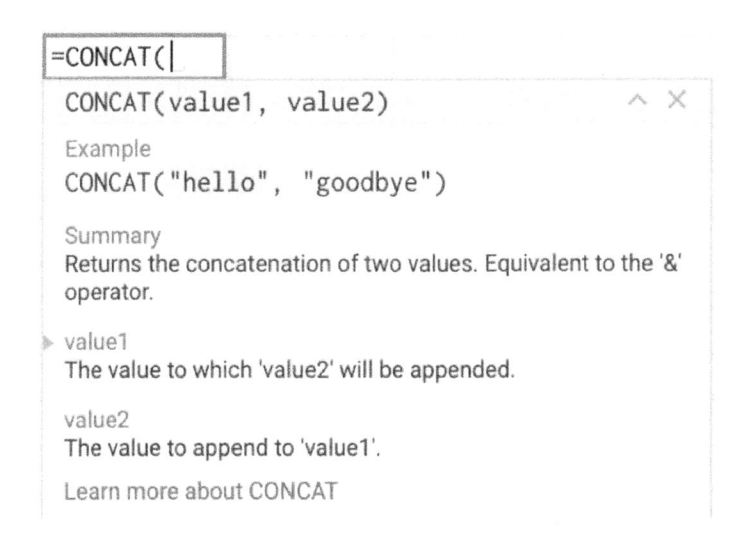

```
=CONCAT(
```

CONCAT(value1, value2)

Example
CONCAT("hello", "goodbye")

Summary
Returns the concatenation of two values. Equivalent to the '&' operator.

value1
The value to which 'value2' will be appended.

value2
The value to append to 'value1'.

Learn more about CONCAT

Note, from Excel 2016, CONCAT now replaces CONCATENATE but CONCATENATE is still backwards compatible with earlier versions of Excel.

## & - AND operator

We can also use the AND operator instead of the CONCATENATE function. In the first example, we had the first name in column A and the last name in column B.

We write the cell reference, then the ampersand symbol(&), add a space (" "), then another ampersand, then the second cell reference:

=A2&" "&B2

Exactly as before it joins the two names together with a space in the middle.

Fred Flintstone

The limitation is that you can't use ranges with the ampersand (&), plus in longer formulas, you have to continually add the ampersand, whereas with the CONCATENATE function you only write it once. Finally, the ampersand is used in other ways and so using it, sometimes can make formulas more difficult to read and understand.

# 5: VLOOKUP (inc IFERROR and ARRAYFORMULA)

Here's how to look up values in tables in Google Sheets using the really useful VLOOKUP function (Vertical Look up). You give it something to look for in the table and it gets the value you're after from a different column in that row.

As always, the best way to show what it does is through examples, showing different aspects and uses of the VLOOKUP function.

## Example 1 - Look up a book number and get the name of who has it

Here we have a list of books, which have an individual reference number, a title and the teacher who is using it. Here we want to find out who has book number 0185. With a small list like this we can easily see who has which book, but imagine a list with hundreds or even thousands of books, that would require looking through from list manually. This is where the VLOOKUP function comes in, as this will deliver the information you need instantly.

|   | A | B | C |
|---|---|---|---|
| 1 | **Number** | **Book** | **Teacher** |
| 2 | 0180 | How Languages Are Learned | John |
| 3 | 0181 | About Language | Paul |
| 4 | 0182 | A-Z of ELT | George |
| 5 | 0183 | Learning one-to-one | Office |
| 6 | 0184 | Classroom Management Techniques | Ringo |
| 7 | 0185 | English for Academic Purposes | John |
| 8 | 0186 | English for Specific Purposes | Office |
| 9 | 0187 | Aligning Tests with the CEFR | Paul |
| 10 | 0188 | Action Research for Language Teachers | George |
| 11 | 0189 | Tasks for Language Teachers | Paul |
| 12 | 0190 | Dictation | Office |
| 13 |   |   |   |
| 14 |   | Book Number: | 0185 |
| 15 |   | Teacher: |   |

We need two things, firstly, a cell to type in the book number we want to find, e.g. C14. Then secondly, a cell to deliver the result, in this case, C15.

In cell C15, we add the VLOOKUP formula. As we can see from the help information, we can see that it requires 4 bits of information.

```
VLOOKUP(search_key, range, index,      ^ ×
[is_sorted])
Example
VLOOKUP(10003, A2:B26, 2, FALSE)
Summary
Vertical lookup. Searches down the first column of a range
for a key and returns the value of a specified cell in the row
found.

search_key
The value to search for. For example, '42', 'Cats' or 'I24'.

range
The range to consider for the search. The first column in the
range is searched for the key specified in 'search_key'.

index
The column index of the value to be returned, where the first
column in 'range' is numbered 1.

is_sorted - [optional]
Indicates whether the column to be searched (the first
column of the specified range) is sorted, in which case the
closest match for 'search_key' will be returned.

Learn more about VLOOKUP

=VLOOKUP(|
```

**search_key**: what we're looking for

**range**: where we should look for the information, often this is the whole table

**index**: which column is the information we're looking for in. The first column of the range, is index 1, the second is index 2, and so on.

**is_sorted**: Is the information we're looking up, i.e. the search info, sorted in order or not? We either put TRUE or FALSE. Another way to look at it is whether you want to find a specific piece of information, i.e. an exact match, or whether it falls within a range (which we're look at in example 3).

So, in this example, we're looking at the contents of cell C14 (book number), looking in the table (range A2:C14), then looking up the value in the third column (teacher in column C), and finally I've stated the range is not sorted as I want an exact match to the book number, i.e. FALSE.

```
=VLOOKUP(C14,A2:C12,3,FALSE)
```

As you can see it's correctly found that John has book number 0185.

|  | Book Number: | 0185 |
|---|---|---|
|  | Teacher: | John |

**Example 2 - Display a message instead of an error, if something cannot be found**

If I tried looking for a book that's not on the list, e.g. book number 0191, it will report an error "#N/A".

|  | A | B | C |
|---|---|---|---|
| 1 | **Number** | **Book** | **Teacher** |
| 2 | 0180 | How Languages Are Learned | John |
| 3 | 0181 | About Language | Paul |
| 4 | 0182 | A-Z of ELT | George |
| 5 | 0183 | Learning one-to-one | Office |
| 6 | 0184 | Classroom Management Techniques | Ringo |
| 7 | 0185 | English for Academic Purposes | John |
| 8 | 0186 | English for Specific Purposes | Office |
| 9 | 0187 | Aligning Tests with the CEFR | Paul |
| 10 | 0188 | Action Research for Language Teachers | George |
| 11 | 0189 | Tasks for Language Teachers | Paul |
| 12 | 0190 | Dictation | Office |
| 13 |  |  |  |
| 14 |  | Book Number: | 0191 |
| 15 |  | Teacher: | #N/A |

If we hover over the error, it will tell us that it couldn't find that book number.

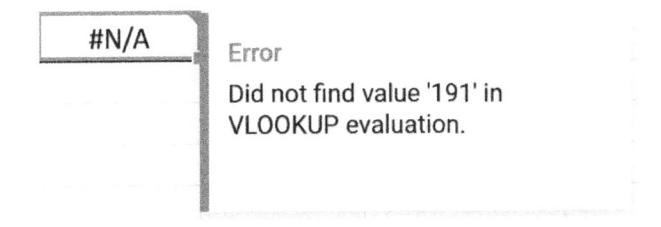

#N/A
Error
Did not find value '191' in VLOOKUP evaluation.

The error looks a little unsightly, and we can modify the VLOOKUP function up so that if it does find an error that it displays a message instead.

To do this, we wrap the VLOOKUP function up in an IFERROR function. Before the VLOOKUP function we type IFERROR then open the brackets. Here it needs two parts, the value (here the VLOOKUP formula), and what to display if it there's an error.

```
=IFERROR(VLOOKUP(C17,A2:C12,3,FALSE),
 IFERROR(value, [value_if_error])
```

After the first part, we add a comma and then for example, write a message we want to display if it finds an error. In this case, let's display "Not found", if it doesn't find the book number. Then we close the brackets, so it's all wrapped up.

```
=IFERROR(VLOOKUP(C17,A2:C12,3,FALSE),"Not found")
```

As we can see the book number in cell C17, hasn't been found and so the message "Not found" appears in C18.

| | |
|---:|:---|
| Book Number: | 0191 |
| Teacher: | Not found |

**Example 3 - Finding values within ranges**

We can also look for values that fall within different ranges. Here we different marks in a level test that correspond to different levels. So, for example, someone who gets 60 in the test, has an advanced level.

| | A | B | C |
|---|---|---|---|
| 1 | Min | Max | Level |
| 2 | 0 | 5 | Elementary |
| 3 | 6 | 15 | Pre-Int |
| 4 | 16 | 25 | Intermediate |
| 5 | 26 | 40 | Upper-Int |
| 6 | 41 | 70 | Advanced |
| 7 | 71 | 100 | Proficiency |
| 8 | | | |
| 9 | Test score: | 20 | |
| 10 | Level: | | |

Here we can set it up to look for the level that corresponds to the test mark in cell B9. So, in the formula, we add the B9 as the search key, the range where the table is (A2:C7), column 3 (level) and this time we state it's TRUE as the value we're looking for is within one of the ranges and not an exact value, so we need to tell Sheets that the ranges are sorted. If we put FALSE, we'll get an error as "20" isn't specifically stated in columns A or B.

```
=VLOOKUP(B9,A2:C7,3,TRUE)
```

Sure enough, it finds that 20 is in between 16 and 25 and therefore the level that corresponds to that is Intermediate.

| 9 | Test score: | 20 |
|---|---|---|
| 10 | Level: | **Intermediate** |

Sometimes it's more convenient to store the reference table on a different sheet.

For example, we use a Google Form connected to a Google Sheet to record level tests completed and the results of the tests appear on one sheet, then using VLOOKUP, the results are compared with the reference table on another sheet.

|   | A | B | C |
|---|---|---|---|
| 1 | **Min** | **Max** | **Level** |
| 2 | 0 | 5 | Elementary |
| 3 | 6 | 15 | Pre-Int |
| 4 | 16 | 25 | Intermediate |
| 5 | 26 | 40 | A4 |
| 6 | 41 | 70 | A5 |
| 7 | 71 | 100 | A6 |

Ref ▼

To do that we modify the formula, so that the sheet name is added to the range. E.g. the table is on the sheet called "Ref" in cells A2:C7, so we write Ref!A2:C7.

`=VLOOKUP(B12,Ref!A2:C7,3,TRUE)`

**Example 4 - Including formulas in a VLOOKUP function**

In the example above, we had already calculated the total mark the student got in a test, then used that total to find their level. We can also do the calculation directly within the VLOOKUP formula.

Here there are four parts of the test, Reading, Listening, Speaking, and Writing. What we want to do is sum those parts then look up the level that corresponds to that total.

|   | A | B | C | D | E |
|---|---|---|---|---|---|
| 1 | **TEST 1** | **Reading** | **Listening** | **Speaking** | **Writing** |
| 2 |  | 4 | 8 | 7 | 5 |

In the search key we add a SUM function, i.e. SUM(F2:I2), which adds up the four parts of the test, that we complete the VLOOKUP formula as before.

5: VLOOKUP (inc IFERROR and ARRAYFORMULA)

```
=VLOOKUP(SUM(B2:E2),Ref!A2:C7,3,TRUE)
```

And again, it finds the correct level.

| 4 | Level: | Intermediate |

**Example 5 - Using wildcards in VLOOKUP**

Sometimes we don't want to state the complete search term we're looking for. For example, here we want to look up a class for a teacher and either we don't want to type in their full name, or maybe we don't know their surname.

Here we have a list of teachers and the classes they have.

|   | A | B |
|---|---|---|
| 1 | **Teachers** | **Classes** |
| 2 | Wilma Flintstone | Jóvenes 1 |
| 3 | Betty Rubble | Junior 2 |
| 4 | Barney Rubble | Junior 3 |
| 5 | Fred Flintstone | Junior 1 |
| 6 |  |  |
| 7 | Teacher's name: | **Betty** |
| 8 | Class name: |  |

We want to find out which class Betty has. Using a normal VLOOKUP formula won't find her as her full name in used in the table. This is where wildcards can be used.

In the search key refer to the cell and add the wildcard symbol "*". This then looks for anything beginning with the name in B7, i.e. the first person it can find with the name Betty. We join the contents of B7 with the wild card by typing B7&"*".

```
=VLOOKUP(B7&"*"
  VLOOKUP(search_key,
  [is_sorted])
```

The rest of the formula is as normal.

```
=VLOOKUP(B7&"*",A2:C5,2,FALSE)
```

5: VLOOKUP (inc IFERROR and ARRAYFORMULA)

Note, if there were two Bettys in the list, it would only find the first one.

There are two wild cards we can use. "*" will ignore any number of characters, and "?" will ignore a single character. So, in this case B7&"?" wouldn't find Betty Rubble.

'?' = single character

'*' = Any number of characters

As we can see it's found Betty's class.

|   | A | B |
|---|---|---|
| 1 | **Teachers** | **Classes** |
| 2 | Wilma Flintstone | Jóvenes 1 |
| 3 | Betty Rubble | Junior 2 |
| 4 | Barney Rubble | Junior 3 |
| 5 | Fred Flintstone | Junior 1 |
| 6 |   |   |
| 7 | Teacher's name: | **Betty** |
| 8 | Class name: | **Junior 2** |

## Example 6 - Looking up multiple values in a table

So far, we've been searching for one thing, but what happens if we want to search for more than one? Well, that's possible too. In this example, we want to find the quantity of a particular product by a particular company, i.e. we're looking for two values then finding the quantity that corresponds to those.

We have two companies (Widgets and Gizmos) and they both sell two products (VR Headsets and Virtual Assistants). We want to find how many VR Headsets Gizmos has.

|   | A | B | C | D |
|---|---|---|---|---|
| 1 | **Company** | **Product** | **Helper Column** | **Quantity** |
| 2 | Widgets Ltd | VR Headsets |   | 30 |
| 3 | Widgets Ltd | Virtual Assistant |   | 40 |
| 4 | Gizmos Ltd | Virtual Assistant |   | 20 |
| 5 | Gizmos Ltd | VR Headsets |   | 50 |
| 6 |   |   |   |   |
| 7 | Company: | **Gizmos Ltd** |   |   |
| 8 | Product: | **VR Headsets** |   |   |
| 9 | Quantity: |   |   |   |

To allow us to look for two values, one of the easiest ways to do this is to create an additional column where we combine the information in the first two columns. So here we've added a 'helper' column in column C, where we join the company and product together. In effect, we're creating one value which we can look up later on.

|   | A | B | C | D |
|---|---|---|---|---|
| 1 | Company | Product | Helper Column | Quantity |
| 2 | Widgets Ltd | VR Headsets | Widgets Ltd VR Headsets | 30 |
| 3 | Widgets Ltd | Virtual Assistant | Widgets Ltd Virtual Assistant | 40 |
| 4 | Gizmos Ltd | Virtual Assistant | Gizmos Ltd Virtual Assistant | 20 |
| 5 | Gizmos Ltd | VR Headsets | Gizmos Ltd VR Headsets | 50 |

In column C, we type the following formula:

=CONCATENATE(A2," ",B2)

As we saw in the CONCATENATE chapter, this gets the value in cell A2 adds a space then adds the value in cell B2. We then copy that formula down column C, so we end up with all the companies and products.

In cell B9, we add the VLOOKUP function. As we are going to allow the user to type in the company in B7 and the product in B8, we need to get those two values and join together, then look for that combined value in the table.

So, our search key is B7 and B8 joined together with a space in the middle, similar to the formula used in the helper column.

=VLOOKUP(B7&" "&B8

VLOOKUP(search_key,
[is_sorted])

Then we add the range, note I've just put columns C and D instead of the whole table. It doesn't make any difference, just remember that when it comes to the index, as I've only selected two columns, the information I'm looking for is in the second column, i.e. index 2.

=VLOOKUP(B7&" "&B8,C2:D5,2, FALSE)

As we can see it's found the correct quantity of Gizmo headsets.

|   | A | B | C | D |
|---|---|---|---|---|
| 1 | Company | Product | Helper Column | Quantity |
| 2 | Widgets Ltd | VR Headsets | Widgets Ltd VR Headsets | 30 |
| 3 | Widgets Ltd | Virtual Assistant | Widgets Ltd Virtual Assistant | 40 |
| 4 | Gizmos Ltd | Virtual Assistant | Gizmos Ltd Virtual Assistant | 20 |
| 5 | Gizmos Ltd | VR Headsets | Gizmos Ltd VR Headsets | 50 |
| 6 |  |  |  |  |
| 7 | Company: | Gizmos Ltd |  |  |
| 8 | Product: | VR Headsets |  |  |
| 9 | Quantity: | 50 |  |  |

## Example 7 - Retrieving multiple values from a table

In a way, this example is the opposite to example 6, in that this time we have one value, a name, and we want to retrieve more than one value from the table.

Here we have some students and their test results across the year. Every semester I need to complete a report and I only want semester 1's results in one report and then semester 2's in the other. I could refer to the individual cells, for example, in the semester 1 report for Ringo, I could write in cell B10, =B5, to get his test 1 result, but of course having to do that for all his tests and then for all the other students is a slow way to do it. Instead, we can use a VLOOKUP formula with an array.

|   | A | B | C | D | E | F | G |
|---|---|---|---|---|---|---|---|
| 1 |  | SEMESTER 1 |  |  | SEMESTER 2 |  |  |
| 2 | Students | Test 1 | Test 2 | Test 3 | Test 4 | Test 5 | Test 6 |
| 3 | John | 67% | 79% | 65% | 78% | 67% | 62% |
| 4 | Paul | 78% | 65% | 77% | 54% | 69% | 75% |
| 5 | Ringo | 88% | 97% | 95% | 87% | 89% | 90% |
| 6 | George | 56% | 78% | 80% | 75% | 55% | 57% |

|   | A | B | C | D |
|---|---|---|---|---|
| 8 |  | SEMESTER 1 |  |  |
| 9 | Student | Test 1 | Test 2 | Test 3 |
| 10 | Ringo |  |  |  |
| 11 |  |  |  |  |
| 12 |  | SEMESTER 2 |  |  |
| 13 | Student | Test 1 | Test 2 | Test 3 |
| 14 | Ringo |  |  |  |

An array in this case, is just telling Sheets how many spaces to the right you want to go to get the value. In the table above, our table goes from column A to G, or if they were numbered it would go from column 1 to 7. So, to get the test results for Ringo for semester 1, we want the cells in columns B, C, and D, or in terms of numbers, 2, 3 and 4.

To do this, we need use the ARRAYFORMULA function along with the VLOOKUP one. All it's doing is allowing us to retrieve more than one value.

In cell B10, we start off with =ARRAYFORMULA then the VLOOKUP function. We refer to A10 (student's name), A3:G6 (the table), then within **CURLY** brackets we add the column numbers we want to retrieve. As stated before, those are columns 2, 3, and 4.

```
=ARRAYFORMULA(VLOOKUP(A10,A3:G6,{2,3,4},FALSE))
```

As we can see it's retrieved the 3 test results from the table. Note, there's no need to type anything in cells C10 or D10, they are filled in automatically.

|   |         | SEMESTER 1 |        |        |
|---|---------|------------|--------|--------|
| 9 | Student | Test 1     | Test 2 | Test 3 |
| 10| Ringo   | 88%        | 97%    | 95%    |

To get Ringo's second semester tests, we use the same formula, except this time we looking in columns 5, 6, and 7 (i.e. columns E, F, and G).

```
=ARRAYFORMULA(VLOOKUP(A10,A3:G6,{5,6,7},FALSE))
```

|    |         | SEMESTER 2 |        |        |
|----|---------|------------|--------|--------|
| 13 | Student | Test 1     | Test 2 | Test 3 |
| 14 | Ringo   | 87%        | 89%    | 90%    |

**Example 8 - Retrieving multiple values from a table (part 2)**

The multiple values we extract from a table don't have to be next to each other as in the example above. We can get them from anywhere along that row.

In this example, the students have done 3 tests and each test has a written component and an oral test. I want to separate their written marks from their oral ones and put them in the tables below.

|   | A | B | C | D | E | F | G |
|---|---|---|---|---|---|---|---|
| 1 |   | TEST 1 || TEST 2 || TEST 3 ||
| 2 | Students | Written | Oral | Written | Oral | Written | Oral |
| 3 | John | 67% | 79% | 65% | 78% | 67% | 62% |
| 4 | Paul | 78% | 65% | 77% | 54% | 69% | 75% |
| 5 | Ringo | 88% | 97% | 95% | 87% | 89% | 90% |
| 6 | George | 56% | 78% | 80% | 75% | 55% | 57% |
| 7 |   |   |   |   |   |   |   |
| 8 |   | Written ||| |||
| 9 | Student | W1 | W2 | W3 | |||
| 10 | Ringo |   |   |   | |||
| 11 |   |   |   |   | |||
| 12 |   | Oral ||| |||
| 13 | Student | O1 | O2 | O3 | |||
| 14 | Ringo |   |   |   | |||

This is just like the example above. We get the student's name from cell I10, look in the table I3:O6, then get the values from columns 2, 4, and 6 (columns J, L, and N).

`=ARRAYFORMULA(VLOOKUP(A10,A3:G6,{2,4,6},FALSE))`

|   | A | B | C | D |
|---|---|---|---|---|
| 8 |   | Written |||
| 9 | Student | W1 | W2 | W3 |
| 10 | Ringo | 88% | 95% | 89% |

Similarly, we can get his oral marks, but this time we get the values from columns 3, 5, and 7 (columns K, M, and O).

`=ARRAYFORMULA(VLOOKUP(A14,A3:G6,{3,5,7},FALSE))`

|   | A | B | C | D |
|---|---|---|---|---|
| 12 |   | Oral |||
| 13 | Student | O1 | O2 | O3 |
| 14 | Ringo | 97% | 87% | 90% |

## Example 9 - Using Named Ranges with VLOOKUP

Sometimes it's useful to name the range in your table, so you know which table you're referring to, particularly if you have more than one in your document. Also, if for some reason there's a chance that the formula will be moved or copied elsewhere, then a Named Range is absolute, i.e. it always refers to the same range even if it's moved.

Looking back at our first example, let's create a Named Range for it.

|   | A | B | C |
|---|---|---|---|
| 1 | Number | Book | Teacher |
| 2 | 0180 | How Languages Are Learned | John |
| 3 | 0181 | About Language | Paul |
| 4 | 0182 | A-Z of ELT | George |
| 5 | 0183 | Learning one-to-one | Office |
| 6 | 0184 | Classroom Management Techniques | Ringo |
| 7 | 0185 | English for Academic Purposes | John |
| 8 | 0186 | English for Specific Purposes | Office |
| 9 | 0187 | Aligning Tests with the CEFR | Paul |
| 10 | 0188 | Action Research for Language Teachers | George |
| 11 | 0189 | Tasks for Language Teachers | Paul |
| 12 | 0190 | Dictation | Office |
| 13 |  |  |  |
| 14 |  | Book Number: | 0185 |
| 15 |  | Teacher: |  |

First, we select the whole table.

|   | A | B | C |
|---|---|---|---|
| 1 | Number | Book | Teacher |
| 2 | 0180 | How Languages Are Learned | John |
| 3 | 0181 | About Language | Paul |
| 4 | 0182 | A-Z of ELT | George |
| 5 | 0183 | Learning one-to-one | Office |
| 6 | 0184 | Classroom Management Techniques | Ringo |
| 7 | 0185 | English for Academic Purposes | John |
| 8 | 0186 | English for Specific Purposes | Office |
| 9 | 0187 | Aligning Tests with the CEFR | Paul |
| 10 | 0188 | Action Research for Language Teachers | George |
| 11 | 0189 | Tasks for Language Teachers | Paul |
| 12 | 0190 | Dictation | Office |

Then right-click and select "Define named range...".

Insert link

Get link to this range

Define named range...

Protect range...

This will open the sidebar where you can name the range and edit it if necessary.

[Named ranges dialog showing "NamedRange1" with range '9'!A1:C12, with Cancel and Done buttons]

Change the default name to something meaningful, for example "BookList". Note, you can't have a name with spaces in it. Then click Done.

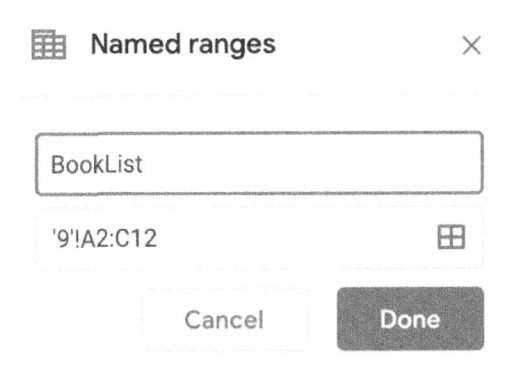

[Named ranges dialog showing "BookList" with range '9'!A2:C12, with Cancel and Done buttons]

Now when we set up the VLOOKUP formula, in the range we just start typing the name of the range. As we type, we will see the named range appear below. Click on it to add it to the formula.

[Formula showing =vlookup(C14,Book with dropdown suggestion "BookList  '9'!A2:C12"]

When we select the named range, we will see the range get highlighted.

```
=vlookup(C14,BookList
```
<br>
VLOOKUP(search_key, range, index, [is_sorted])

| | Number | Book | Teacher |
|---|---|---|---|
| 1 | | | |
| 2 | 0180 | How Languages Are Learned | John |
| 3 | 0181 | About Language | Paul |
| 4 | 0182 | A-Z of ELT | George |
| 5 | 0183 | Learning one-to-one | Office |
| 6 | 0184 | Classroom Management Techniques | Ringo |
| 7 | 0185 | English for Academic Purposes | John |
| 8 | 0186 | English for Specific Purposes | Office |
| 9 | 0187 | Aligning Tests with the CEFR | Paul |
| 10 | 0188 | Action Research for Language Teachers | George |
| 11 | 0189 | Tasks for Language Teachers | Paul |
| 12 | 0190 | Dictation | Office |

The rest is as before and we can see that it works just as first example.

```
=vlookup(C14,BookList,3,FALSE)
```

Say we want to move the book number entry and teacher to a different part of the sheet, this doesn't affect it at all, as it continues to refer to that particular range.

| | A | B | C |
|---|---|---|---|
| 1 | Number | Book | Teacher |
| 2 | 0180 | How Languages Are Learned | John |
| 3 | 0181 | About Language | Paul |
| 4 | 0182 | A-Z of ELT | George |
| 5 | 0183 | Learning one-to-one | Office |
| 6 | 0184 | Classroom Management Techniques | Ringo |
| 7 | 0185 | English for Academic Purposes | John |
| 8 | 0186 | English for Specific Purposes | Office |
| 9 | 0187 | Aligning Tests with the CEFR | Paul |
| 10 | 0188 | Action Research for Language Teachers | George |
| 11 | 0189 | Tasks for Language Teachers | Paul |
| 12 | 0190 | Dictation | Office |
| 13 | | | |
| 14 | | Book Number: | 0185 |
| 15 | | Teacher: | John |

We could do the same by adding dollar signs to the range, to make it an absolute reference and not a relative one.

A couple of final points. The search keys used are **case-insensitive**, so it doesn't matter if you type *betty* or *Betty*, it will find the same result. Here we've looked at Vertical Lookup, but there is also Horizontal Lookup, HLOOKUP, which works in a similar way, and will depend on how your data is set up. However, VLOOKUP is far more common.

# 6: OR & AND (inc WEEKDAY)

With the IF function we usually check if one condition is true or false, but what happens if we want to check multiple conditions? This is where the OR or AND functions come in handy. With OR we can check if one *or* other conditions are true, and with AND we can check if *all* the conditions are true.

We'll start with how the function works then look at some practical examples of both.

**Example 1 - How does the OR function work? And how does it work with IF?**

Let's first look at how the OR function works. Here we have two numbers in cells A1 and A2 and we want to know if *either* number equals 10.

| | A | B |
|---|---|---|
| 1 | 10 | TRUE |
| 2 | 5 | |

In cell B1, we write the following formula:

```
=or(A1=10, A2=10)
```

This looks at the contents of cell A1 and decides if it's equal to 10, and then looks at cell A2 and again decides if it equals to 10. If *either* cell has a 10 in it, then it will display TRUE. If there isn't a 10 in either cell, then it will be FALSE.

So, in the example above, we have a 10 in cell A1, and correctly it displays TRUE in cell B1 meaning that it's found a number 10 in one of the cells.

This is great, but displaying TRUE or FALSE, often doesn't help us very much, and what we want is that if it's TRUE, then the formula does something, and if it's FALSE, it does something else.

So, quite often we wrap up the OR function in an IF function, to allow us to take action depending on whether it's TRUE or FALSE.

So, we modify the formula like this:

=IF(OR(condition 1, condition 2), Action if true, Action if false)

```
=if(or(A1=10,A2=10),"At least one is true", "Both are false")
```

We add IF and an open bracket before the OR function, then after it, we add a comma and the two actions we want to take. In this case, if the function finds a number 10, it displays the text "At least one is true", and if it doesn't, it displays the text "Both are false".

|   | A | B | C |
|---|---|---|---|
| 1 | 10 | TRUE | At least one is true |
| 2 | 5 |   |   |

|   | A | B | C |
|---|---|---|---|
| 1 | 3 | FALSE | Both are false |
| 2 | 5 |   |   |

**Example 2 - Checking to see if at least one race time is below the target time**

Let's use the above formula in a practical example. Here we have some athletes who need to have run under 10.5s in the 100m in two pre-competition races, in order to be able to enter the competition. We have the times they ran in both races, then in column D, we add the OR formula to see if they can compete or not.

|   | A | B | C | D |
|---|---|---|---|---|
| 1 |   | Race 1 | Race 2 | Enter the competition? |
| 2 | Paul | 10.55 | 10.25 | Yes |
| 3 | John | 10.45 | 10.85 | Yes |
| 4 | Ringo | 10.55 | 10.65 | No |
| 5 | George | 10.60 | 10.70 | No |

Here the formula in column D is similar as before, we start with an IF function, then the OR function. Then we add the two conditions, in this case, a check to see if the value in column B is less than 10.5s or if the one in column C is less than 10.5s. If it finds that the athlete has run under 10.5s in one or more of the races, it states "Yes" they can compete in the competition. If they haven't run under 10.5s, then it displays "No".

```
=if(or(B2<10.5,C2<10.5),"Yes", "No")
```

So, we can see that Paul and John are ok to enter the competition.

**Example 3 - Looking at more than two race times**

In the example above we looked at *two* race times, but the OR function can look at lots of different values. Here the athletes have run three races.

|   | A | B | C | D | E |
|---|---|---|---|---|---|
| 1 |   | Race 1 | Race 2 | Race 3 | Enter the competition? |
| 2 | Paul | 10.55 | 10.25 | 10.08 | Yes |
| 3 | John | 10.45 | 10.85 | 11.00 | Yes |
| 4 | Ringo | 10.55 | 10.65 | 10.45 | Yes |
| 5 | George | 10.60 | 10.70 | 10.50 | No |

The formula in column E is as before, except that we just add a third condition in the brackets.

```
=if(or(B2<10.5,C2<10.5,D2<10.5),"Yes", "No")
```

### Example 4 - Using the AND function

The AND function works in a similar way to the OR function. OR looks to see if 1 or more of the conditions are met, whereas, AND checks to see if ALL the conditions are met.

Here we have some students who have to get more than 60% in all three tests on the course, in order to pass the course. If they have, it displays "Passed", if not they haven't it displays "Failed".

|   | A | B | C | D | E |
|---|---|---|---|---|---|
| 1 |   | Test 1 | Test 2 | Test 3 | Passed the course? |
| 2 | Paul | 67% | 78% | 68% | Passed |
| 3 | John | 65% | 54% | 78% | Failed |
| 4 | Ringo | 69% | 70% | 59% | Failed |
| 5 | George | 55% | 54% | 61% | Failed |

In place of the OR function, we add the AND one in column E.

```
=if(AND(B2>0.6, C2>0.6,D2>0.6),"Passed", "Failed")
```

### Example 5 - Using AND to check if the values are within a range

Here we want to see which groups the students should be in. We've already put those who got 80% or more in group 1, and now we want to divide the remaining students into either group 2 or 3. Those who got more than 60% and less than 80% will go in group 2, and the rest will be in group 3.

|   | A | B | C |
|---|---|---|---|
| 1 |   | Test 1 | Group 2 or 3? |
| 2 | Paul | 67% | Group 2 |
| 3 | John | 58% | Group 3 |
| 4 | Ringo | 69% | Group 2 |
| 5 | George | 55% | Group 3 |
| 6 | Fred | 79% | Group 2 |
| 7 | Wilma | 70% | Group 2 |
| 8 | Barney | 61% | Group 2 |
| 9 | Betty | 63% | Group 2 |

To do this, we can use an AND function in column C. We look at the values in column B to see if they are more than 60% or less than 80%. If the test results meet this condition, then it displays "Group 2", otherwise it displays "Group 3".

```
=if(AND(B2>0.6, B2<0.8),"Group 2", "Group 3")
```

**Example 6 - Categorising the values based on certain conditions**

In the example above, we had already allocated some students to Group 1, but this time let's divide up the students into 3 groups all automatically.

|   | A | B | C |
|---|---|---|---|
| 1 |   | Test | Group 1, 2 or 3? |
| 2 | Paul | 67% | Group 2 |
| 3 | John | 58% | Group 3 |
| 4 | Ringo | 85% | Group 1 |
| 5 | George | 55% | Group 3 |
| 6 | Fred | 82% | Group 1 |
| 7 | Wilma | 70% | Group 2 |
| 8 | Barney | 61% | Group 2 |
| 9 | Betty | 63% | Group 2 |

First, in column C we start off with an IF function, and check for those who have 80% or more. If their test result is 80% or more, it displays "Group 1". If the test is less, it moves onto the next IF statement.

This time it checks to see if the result is between 60 and 80%, as we saw in the example above. If it does, then it displays "Group 2", if it doesn't it shows "Group 3".

```
=if(B2>=0.8, "Group 1", if(AND(B2>0.6, B2<0.8),"Group 2", "Group 3"))
```

## Example 7 - Using functions within an OR or AND function

Introducing the WEEKDAY function

We can also use other functions in the OR function. Here we have some prices where if the work was carried out on a weekend, a weekend supplement is added.

We need to check to see if the date fell on a weekend, then based on whether that is TRUE or FALSE, we add a supplement or not.

|    | A     | B        | C       | D              | E           |
|----|-------|----------|---------|----------------|-------------|
| 1  | Date  | Weekend? | Price   | W/E Supplement | Final Price |
| 2  | 12/10 | FALSE    | $30.00  | $10.00         | $30.00      |
| 3  | 14/10 | FALSE    | $40.00  | $10.00         | $40.00      |
| 4  | 19/10 | FALSE    | $30.00  | $10.00         | $30.00      |
| 5  | 20/10 | FALSE    | $25.00  | $10.00         | $25.00      |
| 6  | 21/10 | FALSE    | $30.00  | $10.00         | $30.00      |
| 7  | 22/10 | TRUE     | $40.00  | $10.00         | $50.00      |
| 8  | 23/10 | TRUE     | $50.00  | $10.00         | $60.00      |
| 9  | 24/10 | FALSE    | $25.00  | $10.00         | $25.00      |
| 10 | 28/10 | FALSE    | $20.00  | $10.00         | $20.00      |
| 11 | 30/10 | TRUE     | $30.00  | $10.00         | $40.00      |
| 12 | 31/10 | FALSE    | $30.00  | $10.00         | $30.00      |

In column B, we add this formula:

```
=OR(WEEKDAY(A2)=7, WEEKDAY(A2)=1)
```

The WEEKDAY function looks at the date in column A and converts that into a number between 1 and 7. By default, Sunday is 1 and Saturday is 7. So, if it reports a number that is a 1 or a 7, then the date is at the weekend.

In column E we then check to see if column B is TRUE or FALSE, if it's TRUE we add the supplement, if not, we leave the price as it is.

```
=if(B2=TRUE, C2+D2, C2)
```

We could combine the formulas in columns B and E by wrapping the OR function in an IF one:

So, we have if the date in column A is Saturday (7) or Sunday (1), it adds the price (C) and the supplement (D), if not it just displays the price (C).

```
=if(OR(WEEKDAY(A2)=7, WEEKDAY(A2)=1),C2+D2, C2)
```

Just as a little extra, if we wanted to check to see if it is a *weekday*, we could use an AND function. This checks to see if the date isn't a Saturday (7) and isn't a Sunday (1).

=AND(WEEKDAY(A2)<>7, WEEKDAY(A2)<>1)

# 7: COUNTIF, SUMIF, COUNTIFS, SUMIFS

In this chapter, we're going to look at how we can count things and add things up depending on certain conditions that we set. There are four functions we'll look at here: COUNTIF, SUMIF, COUNTIFS, and SUMIFS.

**Example 1 - COUNTIF: Counting the number of instances of a specific number**

In this example, and to introduce COUNTIF, we have a list of part numbers of some products and we want to know how many parts we have that are numbered "123".

| | A | B |
|---|---|---|
| 1 | Part numbers | Quantity of part 123: |
| 2 | 123 | 6 |
| 3 | 156 | |
| 4 | 145 | |
| 5 | 178 | |
| 6 | 123 | |
| 7 | 178 | |
| 8 | 123 | |
| 9 | 187 | |
| 10 | 165 | |
| 11 | 123 | |
| 12 | 123 | |
| 13 | 124 | |
| 14 | 123 | |
| 15 | 156 | |
| 16 | 178 | |

In cell B2, we write the following formula:

```
=COUNTIF(A2:A16,123)
```

There are two parts, first you state the range of values you want to look at, then in the second part, you state what you want to look for. So, in this case, we're looking in cells A2 to A16 and we are looking for the number 123. As it looks down the row, every time it finds the number 123, it adds it to the count. So, in this example, it found 6 instances of the number 123.

```
COUNTIF(range, criterion)                        ∧ ✕
Example
COUNTIF(A1:A10, ">20")
```

▶ Summary
Returns a conditional count across a range.

range
The range that is tested against 'criterion'.

criterion
The pattern or test to apply to 'range'.

Learn more about COUNTIF

**Example 2 - COUNTIF: Counting how many values are over a certain number**

We can also use COUNTIF to count how many values are greater than or less than a particular number. In fact, it can check against pretty much any type of mathematical condition, an example of which we'll see later.

Here we want to see how many students got over 60 in a test, maybe to divide the group into a stronger one and a weaker one.

|   | A | B | C |
|---|---|---|---|
| 1 | Students | Test results | Number of students with over 60 in test |
| 2 | Paul | 58 | 5 |
| 3 | John | 76 |  |
| 4 | Ringo | 65 |  |
| 5 | George | 59 |  |
| 6 | Wilma | 66 |  |
| 7 | Fred | 98 |  |
| 8 | Betty | 56 |  |
| 9 | Barney | 78 |  |

In cell C2, as before we start off with the COUNTIF function, set the range we want to look at, in this case it's B2 to B9, then set the condition to look for any tests over 60. Notice the syntax of the condition. When we use the operators, like greater than or less than, we have to wrap them up in speech marks.

```
=COUNTIF(B2:B9,">60")
```

And correctly, it's found 5 students with a test result of more than 60.

### Example 3 - COUNTIF: Counting the number of times a word or phrase appears in a range

This time we're going to look for a piece of text. We have a book inventory and we want to know how many books called "English File· we have.

|   | A | B |
|---|---|---|
| 1 | Books | Quantity of the book "English File" |
| 2 | English File | 6 |
| 3 | Cutting Edge | |
| 4 | English File | |
| 5 | SpeakOut | |
| 6 | Cutting Edge | |
| 7 | English FIle | |
| 8 | English File | |
| 9 | SpeakOut | |
| 10 | English File | |
| 11 | Cutting Edge | |
| 12 | english file | |

In cell C2, we write the following formula:

```
=COUNTIF(A2:A12,"English File")
```

Like the operators above, text needs to be in speech marks. Here it's found 6 books called English File.

### Example 4 - COUNTIF: Using a cell reference to find instances of whatever has been written in that cell

So far, we've stated the condition within the formula but often we want a flexible formula that can look for any condition we type in a particular cell.

Here we have the same book inventory but this time we give the user the option to type in the book they are looking for in cell C1. Then in cell C2 it will tell them how many books we have of that name.

|   | A | B | C |
|---|---|---|---|
| 1 | **Books** | **Book Name:** | english file |
| 2 | English File | **Quantity:** | 6 |
| 3 | Cutting Edge | | |
| 4 | English File | | |
| 5 | SpeakOut | | |
| 6 | Cutting Edge | | |
| 7 | English FIle | | |
| 8 | English File | | |
| 9 | SpeakOut | | |
| 10 | English File | | |
| 11 | Cutting Edge | | |
| 12 | english file | | |

In the condition part, the important part and the part where most problems occur, is the syntax here. First, we wrap the equals operator up in speech marks like we saw in example 2. Then to refer to a cell we need to first add the ampersand (&) then the cell reference.

Whatever we type in cell C1, the COUNTIF will look for in the range, making this far more flexible than stating it within the formula.

```
=COUNTIF(A2:A12,"="&C1)
```

**Example 5 - COUNTIF: Using wildcards to look for broader values**

Here we have a list of classes and we want to know how many junior classes we have. The problem is that, there are different levels of Juniors, 1, 2, and 3, so our formulas so far wouldn't be able to find all these different ones. That's where a wildcard comes in.

|   | A | B |
|---|---|---|
| 1 | **Classes** | **Number of Junior classes** |
| 2 | Junior 1 | 8 |
| 3 | Junior 2 | |
| 4 | Junior 3 | |
| 5 | Jóvenes 1 | |
| 6 | Jóvenes 2 | |
| 7 | Jóvenes 3 | |
| 8 | Junior 1 | |
| 9 | Junior 1 | |
| 10 | Junior 2 | |
| 11 | Junior 2 | |
| 12 | Junior 3 | |
| 13 | Jóvenes 1 | |
| 14 | Jóvenes 2 | |

In cell B2, we type the following formula:

```
=COUNTIF(A2:A14,"Junior*")
```

The key part here, is the use of the asterisk (*) after the word Junior. This allows it to look for anything that starts with the word Junior and it doesn't matter what comes afterwards. Hence it will count the number of times there is a class starting with the word Junior. In this case, there are 8.

The wildcard can also be used before the word, for example, you could look for all the classes in level 1, by typing "*1", which would look for anything ending in 1.

**Example 6 - COUNTIF: Counting dates**

The final example of COUNTIF, shows us that we can also count the number of times a date appears. For example, here we want to know how many appointments we have on 17/10/2016.

| | A | B | C |
|---|---|---|---|
| 1 | Date | Time | Appointments on 17/10 |
| 2 | 17/10/2016 | 10:00 | 6 |
| 3 | 17/10/2016 | 10:30 | |
| 4 | 19/10/2016 | 10:00 | |
| 5 | 21/10/2016 | 10:00 | |
| 6 | 17/10/2016 | 11:00 | |
| 7 | 20/10/2016 | 10:30 | |
| 8 | 21/10/2016 | 11:30 | |
| 9 | 17/10/2016 | 11:30 | |
| 10 | 19/10/2016 | 10:30 | |
| 11 | 18/10/2016 | 10:00 | |
| 12 | 17/10/2016 | 12:00 | |
| 13 | 18/10/2016 | 11:00 | |
| 14 | 18/10/2016 | 12:00 | |
| 15 | 17/10/2016 | 12:30 | |

Dates like text, need to be in speech marks. It's also important to match the format. I usually state the day, month and year, even if the dates in the table are formatted in a different way. I.e. if the data just showed the day and month, the formula would still work.

```
=COUNTIF(A2:A15,"17/10/2016")
```

# Example 7 - SUMIF: Adding up the number of products sold on a particular date

Now let's look at SUMIF. This is similar to COUNTIF but the syntax can be slightly different as quite often we're not looking at just one range.

Here we have some products that have been sold on different days and we have how many of each product has been sold. What we want to know is how many products did we sell on a particular date, e.g. 17/10. In cell E1, the user types in the date they want to find the information for, then in cell E2, it will tell us how many have been sold.

|    | A          | B        | C             | D             | E          |
|----|------------|----------|---------------|---------------|------------|
| 1  | Date       | Products | Quantity sold | Date:         | 17/10/2016 |
| 2  | 16/10/2016 | ABC      | 200           | Quantity sold:| 1000       |
| 3  | 17/10/2016 | ABC      | 100           |               |            |
| 4  | 17/10/2016 | XYZ      | 300           |               |            |
| 5  | 18/10/2016 | XYZ      | 150           |               |            |
| 6  | 19/10/2016 | ABC      | 200           |               |            |
| 7  | 17/10/2016 | DEF      | 600           |               |            |
| 8  | 18/10/2016 | ABC      | 200           |               |            |
| 9  | 18/10/2016 | DEF      | 300           |               |            |
| 10 | 19/10/2016 | DEF      | 450           |               |            |
| 11 | 19/10/2016 | XYZ      | 100           |               |            |
| 12 | 20/10/2016 | ABC      | 250           |               |            |

In the brackets, we first type the range where we're looking for the date, e.g. A2 to A12. Then we add the criteria, in this case whatever's in cell E1 (the date). Then for SUMIF, we add a third part, this is the range which contains the values we going to sum, e.g. quantities sold ('sum range').

```
=SUMIF(A2:A12,E1,C2:C12)
```

SUMIF(range, criterion, [sum_range])

Example
SUMIF(A1:A10, ">20", B1:B10)

Summary
Returns a conditional sum across a range.

range
The range which is tested against 'criterion'.

criterion
The pattern or test to apply to 'range'.

sum_range - [optional]
The range to be added up, if different from 'range'.

Learn more about SUMIF

So, in our example, it's found 3 dates that equal the 17/10 and summed up the quantities sold on those dates, i.e. 100+300+600 = 1,000.

**Example 8 - SUMIFS: To find the quantity sold within a date range**

Similar to SUMIF, we have the function SUMIFS, which uses more than one criterion before adding up. Here we have the same information as before, but this time we want to find out how many products we've sold between two dates (17/10 to 19/10).

|    | A | B | C | D | E |
|---|---|---|---|---|---|
| 1 | Date | Products | Quantity sold | Start date: | 17/10/2016 |
| 2 | 16/10/2016 | ABC | 200 | Finish date: | 19/10/2016 |
| 3 | 17/10/2016 | ABC | 100 | Quantity sold: | 2400 |
| 4 | 17/10/2016 | XYZ | 300 | | |
| 5 | 18/10/2016 | XYZ | 150 | | |
| 6 | 19/10/2016 | ABC | 200 | | |
| 7 | 17/10/2016 | DEF | 600 | | |
| 8 | 18/10/2016 | ABC | 200 | | |
| 9 | 18/10/2016 | DEF | 300 | | |
| 10 | 19/10/2016 | DEF | 450 | | |
| 11 | 19/10/2016 | XYZ | 100 | | |
| 12 | 20/10/2016 | ABC | 250 | | |

Important: The syntax here is different from SUMIF, and let's go through it step by step.

```
SUMIFS(sum_range, criteria_range1,
criterion1, [criteria_range2, ...],
[criterion2, ...])
```

Example
SUMIFS(A1:A10, B1:B10, ">20", C1:C10, "<30")

Summary
Returns the sum of a range depending on multiple criteria.

sum_range
The range to sum.

criteria_range1
The range to check against criterion1.

criterion1
The pattern or test to apply to criteria_range1.

criteria_range2... - [optional] repeatable
Additional ranges to check.

criterion2... - [optional] repeatable
Additional criteria to check.

Learn more about SUMIFS

`=SUMIFS(C2:C12,A2:A12,">="&E1,A2:A12,"<="&E2)`

We start with the range we want to get the values from, i.e. the sum range (C2:C12).

Then we state the range we want to find the dates in, i.e. A2:A12.

Then the first criteria we want to use, i.e. the date is greater than or equal to the date in cell E1, in this case, 17/10/2016 (">="&E1). As before the operator is in speech marks, and the cell reference has an ampersand before it.

Then we add the second condition. In this example, the range is the same, i.e. A2:A12.

Then we want to look for dates less than or equal to the date in cell E2, in this case, 19/10/2016 ("<="&E2).

It then adds up the products sold between those dates,

100+300+150+200+600+200+300+450+100 = 2,400.

It looks a fairly complicated formula but it really just has three parts:

sum range, criteria 1 (range & criteria), criteria 2 (range & criteria)

We can add more criteria if we want just by adding another range and criteria on the end.

### Example 9 - COUNTIF: Counting how many students are above average

Returning back to COUNTIF, we can use other functions as the criteria within the COUNTIF one.

Here we want to see how many students got over the average mark in an exam. Normally, we would have to find the average of all the marks, then see which marks were above that figure. Well, that's exactly what the COUNTIF function can do for you.

|   | A | B | C |
|---|---|---|---|
| 1 | Students | Exam mark | Number of students above average |
| 2 | John | 65% | 4 |
| 3 | Paul | 68% | |
| 4 | Ringo | 75% | |
| 5 | George | 76% | |
| 6 | Fred | 63% | |
| 7 | Wilma | 76% | |
| 8 | Betty | 70% | |
| 9 | Barney | 60% | |

In the second part, we want to know what marks are greater than the average of all the marks in that range. So, we start off with the greater than operator in speech marks, then like the cell referencing we need to add an ampersand before the function AVERAGE. Then we add the range we want to average.

=COUNTIF(B2:B9,">"&AVERAGE(B2:B9))

The average was 69%, and so correctly it's found that 4 students got an above average mark.

**Example 10 - COUNTIFS: Highlighting duplicate rows**

In this final example, we can use the COUNTIFS function in conjunction with conditional formatting, to highlight rows on our sheet which have duplicate information.

Here we have a list of classes, their timetables and teachers. Some of the rows are duplicates and we can use COUNTIFS to find the duplicates. We add a fourth column to record if the row is duplicate or not.

|    | A | B | C | D |
|----|---|---|---|---|
| 1  | Class | Timetable | Teacher | Duplicate? |
| 2  | Junior 1 | TT 17:00 | Gloria | TRUE |
| 3  | Junior 1 | MW 17:00 | Phil | FALSE |
| 4  | Junior 2 | MW 18:00 | Claire | FALSE |
| 5  | Junior 2 | TT 18:00 | Jay | FALSE |
| 6  | Junior 1 | TT 17:00 | Gloria | TRUE |
| 7  | Junior 2 | MW 17:00 | Phil | TRUE |
| 8  | Junior 2 | MW 18:00 | Luke | FALSE |
| 9  | Junior 2 | TT 17:00 | Hayley | FALSE |
| 10 | Junior 1 | MW 17:00 | Gloria | FALSE |
| 11 | Junior 2 | MW 17:00 | Phil | TRUE |
| 12 | Junior 2 | MW 19:00 | Claire | FALSE |
| 13 | Junior 2 | TT 17:00 | Jay | FALSE |

In column D, we add the following formula:

=COUNTIFS($A$2:$A$13,$A2,$B$2:$B$13,$B2,$C$2:$C$13,$C2)>1

It works by looking in the 3 columns A, B, and C and sees if there is more than 1 occurrence of the contents of that row. So, taking the first row (row 2) as an example:

It checks to see if the content of cell A2, B2, and C2 occurs more than once in the rows below, which it does, i.e. in row 6. So, it states that it's TRUE that it occurs more than once, in other words, it's duplicated.

If we look at row 3, we can see that this time that the combination of those three pieces of information are not repeated in the other rows. So, it states that it's FALSE that it occurs more than once.

We could leave it like that and if we wanted to remove the duplicates or edit them, we just look for those rows which have TRUE in them. However, to make it easier to find them, we can colour the rows to highlight them.

Having selected the contents of the table (range A2:A13), right-click and select "Conditional Formatting..." from the menu.

|   | A | B | C | D |
|---|---|---|---|---|
| 1 | **Class** | **Timetable** | **Teacher** | **Duplicate?** |
| 2 | Junior 1 | TT 17:00 | Gloria | TRUE |
| 3 | Junior 1 | MW 17:00 | Phil | FALSE |
| 4 | Junior 2 | MW 18:00 | Claire | FALSE |
| 5 | Junior 2 | TT 18:00 | Jay | FALSE |
| 6 | Junior 1 | TT 17:00 | Gloria | TRUE |
| 7 | Junior 2 | MW 17:00 | Phil | TRUE |
| 8 | Junior 2 | MW 18:00 | Luke | FALSE |
| 9 | Junior 2 | TT 17:00 | Hayley | FALSE |
| 10 | Junior 1 | MW 17:00 | Gloria | FALSE |
| 11 | Junior 2 | MW 17:00 | Phil | TRUE |
| 12 | Junior 2 | MW 19:00 | Claire | FALSE |
| 13 | Junior 2 | TT 17:00 | Jay | FALSE |

Insert note

Conditional formatting...

Data validation...

This opens the Conditional format rules sidebar menu. Click on the drop-down menu, which by default says "Cell is not empty".

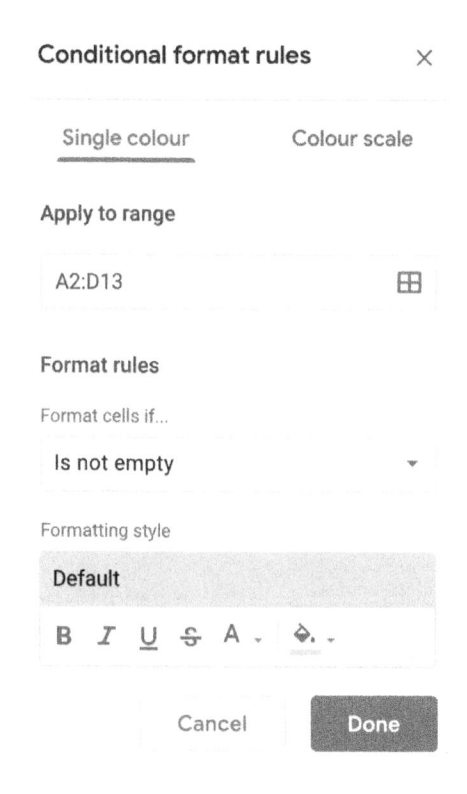

**Conditional format rules**  ×

Single colour    Colour scale

**Apply to range**

A2:D13

**Format rules**

Format cells if...

Is not empty

Formatting style

Default

B  I  U  S  A.  ◇.

Cancel    **Done**

Then scroll down to the bottom of the menu and select "Custom formula is".

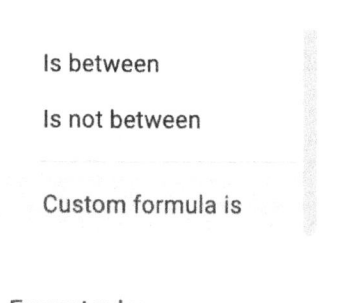

Is between

Is not between

Custom formula is

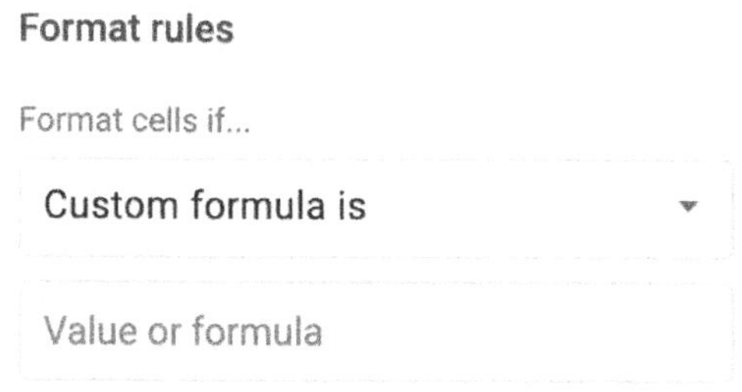

**Format rules**

Format cells if...

Custom formula is

Value or formula

In the box where it says "Value or formula", type in the formula below:

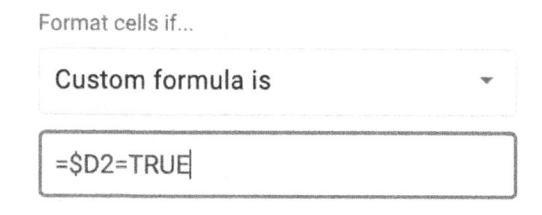

Format cells if...

Custom formula is

=$D2=TRUE

64                                  7: COUNTIF, SUMIF, COUNTIFS, SUMIFS

Click OK and this adds the conditional format rule to the range.

**Conditional format rules**

123  Custom formula is
=$D2=TRUE
A2:D13

This checks to see if the value in column D is TRUE. If it is, it adds the formatting to the whole line.

|    | A | B | C | D |
|----|---|---|---|---|
| 1  | **Class** | **Timetable** | **Teacher** | **Duplicate?** |
| 2  | Junior 1 | TT 17:00 | Gloria | TRUE |
| 3  | Junior 1 | MW 17:00 | Phil | FALSE |
| 4  | Junior 2 | MW 18:00 | Claire | FALSE |
| 5  | Junior 2 | TT 18:00 | Jay | FALSE |
| 6  | Junior 1 | TT 17:00 | Gloria | TRUE |
| 7  | Junior 2 | MW 17:00 | Phil | TRUE |
| 8  | Junior 2 | MW 18:00 | Luke | FALSE |
| 9  | Junior 2 | TT 17:00 | Hayley | FALSE |
| 10 | Junior 1 | MW 17:00 | Gloria | FALSE |
| 11 | Junior 2 | MW 17:00 | Phil | TRUE |
| 12 | Junior 2 | MW 19:00 | Claire | FALSE |
| 13 | Junior 2 | TT 17:00 | Jay | FALSE |

# 8: FILTER

Here we're going to look at the FILTER function. But you can add a filter to a table via the filter option in the menu, I hear you cry! You can, but the FILTER function allows you to put those filtered results on a different part of your page or on a different sheet, and thus, not affect the original table. It also allows for more complex filtering, which the filter option in the menu doesn't offer.

Here are some examples showing you the various uses of the FILTER function and how it can also be combined with other functions, to filter out the information you need, in one single formula.

**Example 1 - Filtering a list by a piece of text**

Here we have a list of companies and the products they sell. I want to a list of the ones only Widgets Ltd sell.

|   | A | B |
|---|---|---|
| 1 | Company | Product |
| 2 | Gizmos Ltd | ABC123 |
| 3 | Gizmos Ltd | ABC321 |
| 4 | Gizmos Ltd | ABC345 |
| 5 | Widgets Ltd | XYZ123 |
| 6 | Widgets Ltd | XYZ321 |
| 7 | Widgets Ltd | XYZ345 |
| 8 | Coolstuff Ltd | EFG123 |
| 9 | Coolstuff Ltd | EFG321 |
| 10 | Whizzbang Ltd | DEF123 |
| 11 | Whizzbang Ltd | DEF321 |
| 12 | Whizzbang Ltd | DEF345 |

I want to leave the original list untouched, so I put my FILTER function on a different part of the page, for example, in cell D2. First, I put the same headers as the original list (just by copying and pasting).

| D | E |
|---|---|
| Company | Product |
|   |   |

Then in cell D2, I write the following FILTER function:

`=filter(A1:B12,A1:A12="Widgets Ltd")`

This looks at the range A1:B12 (i.e. the data in the original table), then shows anything that matches the condition. In this case, it's looking in column A (A1:A12) and shows anything that matches the name "Widgets Ltd". Note, the use of speech marks for text.

It then automatically lists just those products that Widgets Ltd sells.

| Company | Product |
|---|---|
| Widgets Ltd | XYZ123 |
| Widgets Ltd | XYZ321 |
| Widgets Ltd | XYZ345 |

## Example 2 - Filtering a list by those who still need to pay

An academy has a list of students, the cost of their course and how much they still need to pay. Here I want to make a list of those who still need to pay, so we can contact them.

| | A | B | C |
|---|---|---|---|
| 1 | Student | Course cost | Money to pay |
| 2 | Paul McDonald | €500.00 | €500.00 |
| 3 | Ringo Stardust | €500.00 | €0.00 |
| 4 | George Harris | €600.00 | €200.00 |
| 5 | John London | €800.00 | €400.00 |
| 6 | Fred Flintshire | €400.00 | €0.00 |
| 7 | Wilma Flintrock | €500.00 | €0.00 |
| 8 | Betty Rubles | €400.00 | €200.00 |
| 9 | Barney Rudder | €600.00 | €600.00 |
| 10 | Jay Pitchfork | €500.00 | €0.00 |
| 11 | Claire Doneful | €500.00 | €0.00 |
| 12 | Gloria Thinn | €400.00 | €100.00 |

I put the headers in columns E to G.

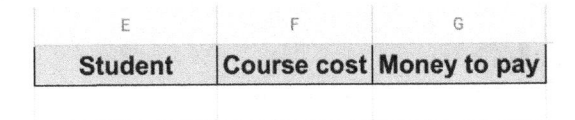

| E | F | G |
|---|---|---|
| Student | Course cost | Money to pay |

Then in cell E2, I write the following FILTER function:

```
=filter(A2:C12,C2:C12>0)
```

Here I'm looking at the range A2:C12. Note, it's usually better to not include the header in the range, i.e. not A1.

Then, I want to know who hasn't paid, which will be anyone who has more than 0 euros to pay in column C. So, I write the range C2:C12 and state anything more than 0.

This then makes a list of those who still need to pay for their course.

| Student | Course cost | Money to pay |
|---|---|---|
| Paul McDonald | €500.00 | €500.00 |
| George Harris | €600.00 | €200.00 |
| John London | €800.00 | €400.00 |
| Betty Rubles | €400.00 | €200.00 |
| Barney Rudder | €600.00 | €600.00 |
| Gloria Thinn | €400.00 | €100.00 |

## Example 3 - Filtering a table by a specific date

Here we have a list of appointments, with the date, time and person's name.

| | A | B | C |
|---|---|---|---|
| 1 | Date | Time | Name |
| 2 | 24/10 | 10:00 | Paul McDonald |
| 3 | 24/10 | 11:00 | Ringo Stardust |
| 4 | 25/10 | 10:00 | George Harris |
| 5 | 26/10 | 10:00 | John London |
| 6 | 27/10 | 10:00 | Fred Flintshire |
| 7 | 26/10 | 11:00 | Wilma Flintrock |
| 8 | 24/10 | 12:00 | Betty Rubles |
| 9 | 24/10 | 13:00 | Barney Rudder |
| 10 | 25/10 | 11:00 | Jay Pitchfork |
| 11 | 24/10 | 14:00 | Claire Doneful |
| 12 | 26/10 | 12:00 | Gloria Thinn |

I want to filter the table to just show those appointments on 24/10.

| E | F | G | H |
|---|---|---|---|
| Date | Time | Name | 24/10 |
| 24/10 | 10:00 | Paul McDonald | |
| 24/10 | 11:00 | Ringo Stardust | |
| 24/10 | 12:00 | Betty Rubles | |
| 24/10 | 13:00 | Barney Rudder | |
| 24/10 | 14:00 | Claire Doneful | |

In cell E2, I write the following FILTER function:

```
=filter(A2:C12,A2:A12=H1)
```

It looks at the table (A2 to C12) and then looks at column A to find dates that match the date in cell H1, i.e. 24/10.

I could also find out the appointments I have today, by just adding the TODAY() function instead of the cell reference:

`=filter(A2:C12,A2:A12=today())`

This then displays just the appointments with today's date.

### Example 4 - Filtering a table between two dates

Here we have the attendance of a particular group of 6 students for the period between 3/10 and 21/10. I want to show the attendance between two dates.

|   | A | B | C | D | E | F | G |
|---|---|---|---|---|---|---|---|
| 1 |   |   |   | Students |   |   |   |
| 2 | Date | PM | RS | GH | JL | FF | BR |
| 3 | 3/10 | X | X | X | X | X | X |
| 4 | 4/10 |   | X | X | X | X |   |
| 5 | 5/10 | X |   | X | X | X | X |
| 6 | 6/10 | X |   | X | X | X | X |
| 7 | 7/10 | X | X | X |   | X |   |
| 8 | 10/10 | X |   | X | X | X | X |
| 9 | 11/10 | X | X | X | X | X |   |
| 10 | 12/10 | X | X |   | X | X | X |
| 11 | 13/10 | X | X | X | X | X | X |
| 12 | 14/10 | X |   | X | X | X | X |
| 13 | 17/10 | X | X | X |   | X | X |
| 14 | 18/10 |   |   | X | X | X |   |
| 15 | 19/10 | X |   | X | X | X | X |
| 16 | 20/10 |   |   |   | X | X | X |
| 17 | 21/10 | X | X | X | X | X | X |

To the side, I set up my filtered list, with the same headers as the original list, plus I want to be able to type in the date range (i.e. start and finish date), so I add that in columns P & Q.

| I | J | K | L | M | N | O | P | Q |
|---|---|---|---|---|---|---|---|---|
|   |   |   | Students |   |   |   | START DATE: | 10/10 |
| Date | PM | RS | GH | JL | FF | BR | FINISH DATE: | 16/10 |
| 10/10 | X |   | X | X | X | X |   |   |
| 11/10 | X | X | X | X | X |   |   |   |
| 12/10 | X | X |   | X | X | X |   |   |
| 13/10 | X | X | X | X | X | X |   |   |
| 14/10 | X |   | X | X | X | X |   |   |

In cell I3 I write the following FILTER function:

=FILTER(A3:G17,A3:A17>=Q1, A3:A17<=Q2)

This looks at the range A3 to G17 (the original list), then filters by two conditions.

The first looks in column A (the dates) and shows anything that is equal to or greater than the date set in cell Q1 (i.e. 10/10).

The second looks in column A and shows anything that is equal to or less than the date set in cell Q2 (i.e. 16/10). So, effectively it's looking for dates between 10/10 and 16/10.

It then shows just those rows that meet the criteria.

**Example 5 - Filtering a table by a specific month**

Here we've got a similar situation to the one before, where we have the attendance of a group of students. This time they have attended class across 3 different months, October, November, and December.

|   | A | B | C | D | E | F | G |
|---|---|---|---|---|---|---|---|
| 1 |   |   |   | Students |   |   |   |
| 2 | Date | PM | RS | GH | JL | FF | BR |
| 3 | 3/10 | X | X | X | X | X | X |
| 4 | 4/10 |   | X | X | X | X |   |
| 5 | 5/10 | X |   | X | X | X | X |
| 6 | 6/10 | X |   | X | X | X | X |
| 7 | 7/10 | X | X | X |   | X |   |
| 8 | 7/11 | X |   | X | X | X | X |
| 9 | 8/11 | X | X | X | X | X |   |
| 10 | 9/11 | X | X |   | X | X | X |
| 11 | 10/11 | X | X | X | X | X | X |
| 12 | 11/11 | X |   | X | X | X | X |
| 13 | 5/12 | X | X | X |   | X | X |
| 14 | 6/12 |   |   | X | X | X |   |
| 15 | 7/12 | X |   | X | X | X | X |
| 16 | 8/12 |   |   |   | X | X | X |
| 17 | 9/12 | X | X | X | X | X | X |

I want to filter the information so that it just shows the attendance for November. So, first I set up a place to show the filtered results by copying the first two rows from the original list.

8: FILTER

| Date | PM | RS | GH | JL | FF | BR |
|---|---|---|---|---|---|---|
| | | | Students | | | |
| 7/11 | X | | x | X | X | X |
| 8/11 | X | x | X | X | X | |
| 9/11 | X | X | | X | X | X |
| 10/11 | X | X | X | X | X | X |
| 11/11 | X | | X | X | X | X |

Then in cell I3, I add the following FILTER function:

`=filter(A3:G17,month(A3:A17)=11)`

This looks in the table (A3 to G17) and then looks for a month in column A that equals the 11th month, i.e. November.

In case you haven't come across the MONTH function before, this returns the month number from a date, so, January is 1 and December is 12, etc.

As we can see it gets just those rows which are in November.

### Example 6 - Counting the number of values that meet the filter condition

This time instead of returning the actual filtered data, we're going to count how many times the data in the table meets our criteria.

We have similar data to what we saw in Example 2, where we have a list of students, this time with the course month they want, and how much they still need to pay.

| | A | B | C |
|---|---|---|---|
| 1 | **Student** | **Course** | **Money to pay** |
| 2 | Paul McDonald | Sep | €500.00 |
| 3 | Ringo Stardust | Sep | €0.00 |
| 4 | George Harris | Oct | €200.00 |
| 5 | John London | Oct | €400.00 |
| 6 | Fred Flintshire | Oct | €0.00 |
| 7 | Wilma Flintrock | Nov | €0.00 |
| 8 | Betty Rubles | Nov | €200.00 |
| 9 | Barney Rudder | Nov | €600.00 |
| 10 | Jay Pitchfork | Dec | €0.00 |
| 11 | Claire Doneful | Dec | €0.00 |
| 12 | Gloria Thinn | Dec | €100.00 |

I want to find out how many students still need to pay for the November course. So, to the side, I set up a place to enter the month I want (cell F1) and where the result will appear (cell F2).

| E | F |
|---|---|
| Course month: | Nov |
| Number to pay: | 2 |

In cell F2, I write the following FILTER function combining it with the COUNT function:

```
=count(filter(A2:C12,B2:B12=F1, C2:C12>0))
```

Let's first look at the FILTER part. This looks at the table (A2 to C12), then looks to see if two criteria have been met.

Firstly, do the months in column B equal the month in cell F1 (i.e. November)? Secondly, are the figures in column C over 0€? If both criteria are met then it returns a match.

This would normally, display the 2 matches, but I've surrounded the FILTER function in a COUNT one, which will just return the number of matches, in this case, two.

The use of this is similar to that of COUNTIF, which we saw in the last chapter.

### Example 7 - Summing up the total of values that meet the filter condition

Using the same data, this time I want to find out how much in total is still to be paid for the November courses. Instead of using the COUNT function I'll use the SUM one.

| | A | B | C |
|---|---|---|---|
| 1 | **Student** | **Course** | **Money to pay** |
| 2 | Paul McDonald | Sep | €500.00 |
| 3 | Ringo Stardust | Sep | €0.00 |
| 4 | George Harris | Oct | €200.00 |
| 5 | John London | Oct | €400.00 |
| 6 | Fred Flintshire | Oct | €0.00 |
| 7 | Wilma Flintrock | Nov | €0.00 |
| 8 | Betty Rubles | Nov | €200.00 |
| 9 | Barney Rudder | Nov | €600.00 |
| 10 | Jay Pitchfork | Dec | €0.00 |
| 11 | Claire Doneful | Dec | €0.00 |
| 12 | Gloria Thinn | Dec | €100.00 |

I enter the month I want in cell F1 as before.

| | E | F |
|---|---|---|
| | Course month: | Nov |
| | Amount to pay: | €800.00 |

This time I just want to look in column C, as that's where the figures I need to add up are. Then it needs to look in column B and find any months which match the month in cell F1, i.e. November.

Finally, I surround it all in a SUM function to add up the money that is still to be paid for the November courses, i.e. 0€ + 200€ + 600€ = 800€.

`=SUM(filter(C2:C12,B2:B12=F1))`

Note, here we don't need to worry about the values in column C being 0, as adding these up won't make any difference to the total.

The use of this is similar to that of SUMIF.

**Example 8 - Filtering a table using one criterion OR another**

In examples 4 and 6, we looked for data that met BOTH criteria. In this final example, we're going to see how we can look for data that meets one criterion OR another.

Here we have a list of classes and teachers. In column A, we have the level name, column B the different groups for that level, and the teachers who are teaching those classes.

| | A | B | C |
|---|---|---|---|
| 1 | **Classes** | **Group** | **Teachers** |
| 2 | Junior 1 | A | Ed |
| 3 | Junior 1 | B | Colin |
| 4 | Junior 1 | C | Roxanne |
| 5 | Junior 2 | A | Mark |
| 6 | Junior 2 | B | Chris |
| 7 | Junior 2 | C | Scott |
| 8 | Junior 2 | D | Karl |
| 9 | Junior 3 | A | Glyn |
| 10 | Junior 3 | B | Colin |
| 11 | Junior 3 | C | Mark |
| 12 | Junior 3 | D | Chris |
| 13 | Senior 1 | A | Ed |
| 14 | Senior 1 | B | Roxanne |
| 15 | Senior 1 | C | Laura |
| 16 | Senior 2 | A | Karl |
| 17 | Senior 2 | B | Glyn |
| 18 | Senior 3 | A | Jane |

I want to list just the Junior 1 and 3 classes. So, in columns E, F, and G I set up a place to put the filtered responses.

| Classes | Group | Teachers |
|---------|-------|----------|
| Junior 1 | A | Ed |
| Junior 1 | B | Colin |
| Junior 1 | C | Roxanne |
| Junior 3 | A | Glyn |
| Junior 3 | B | Colin |
| Junior 3 | C | Mark |
| Junior 3 | D | Chris |

Then in cell E2, I write the following FILTER function:

`=filter(A2:C18,(A2:A18="Junior 1")+(A2:A18="Junior 3"))`

This looks at the table (A2 to C18), then looks for data that meets 1 of 2 criteria. Firstly, in column A it's looking for levels that are called Junior 1 and secondly, in column A, levels that are called Junior 3.

The important thing here is the plus sign between the two criteria. This means that it will display any row that has the level Junior 1 OR Junior 3.

Further notes and tips

You may have noticed that when the filtered results are returned, only the values are returned and the formatting is not copied. So, sometimes afterwards you will need to add borders, colours, etc to the filtered results.

Also, sometimes you may get an error message instead of returned results. This is sometimes because you've not left enough blank space below the filter cell for the results. It won't overwrite any cells that aren't empty, it will just return an #REF! error. So, make sure you put your FILTER function where there is plenty of space below it.

If you decide to put your filtered results on a different page, you will need to include the sheet name in your formulas. For example, if the main table is on Sheet 1, in the first part of the formula, I write Sheet1!A1:1B12, which refers to that range on Sheet 1.

`=filter(Sheet1!A1:B12,A1:A12="Widgets Ltd")`

# 9: IMPORTRANGE

Google Sheets has a wonderfully useful function called IMPORTRANGE. So, what does it do? It allows you to connect different spreadsheets and import data from one to another. The most basic example would be to connect one sheet with another sheet and import some data from the first sheet to the second.

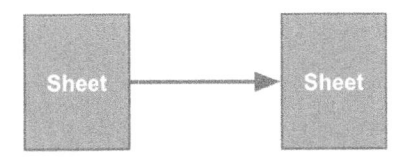

What's important is that if you change the data in the first sheet, it's **automatically updates** in the second sheet.

Not only can you connect two spreadsheets, but you can connect multiple spreadsheets with a master sheet. This can be useful if, for example, you only want someone to see part of the data you have on the master sheet, so you share the individual sheet or range with them.

Either the master is updated and the information is sent out to the individual sheets.

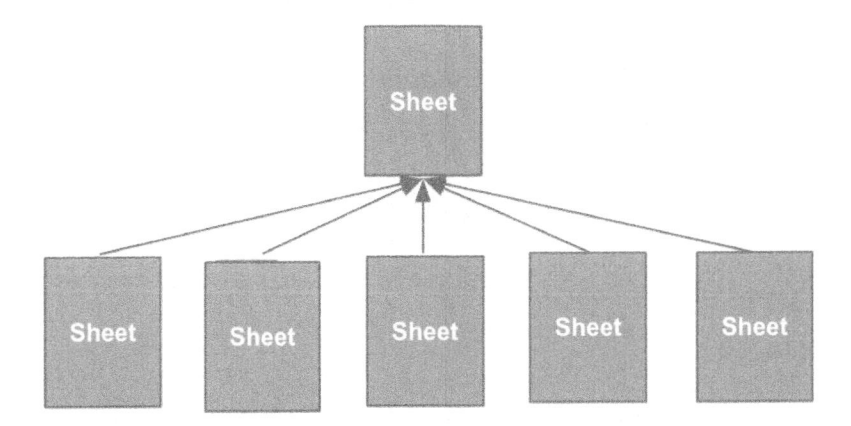

Or you can have the opposite, users update the individual sheets and the information is sent to the master sheet.

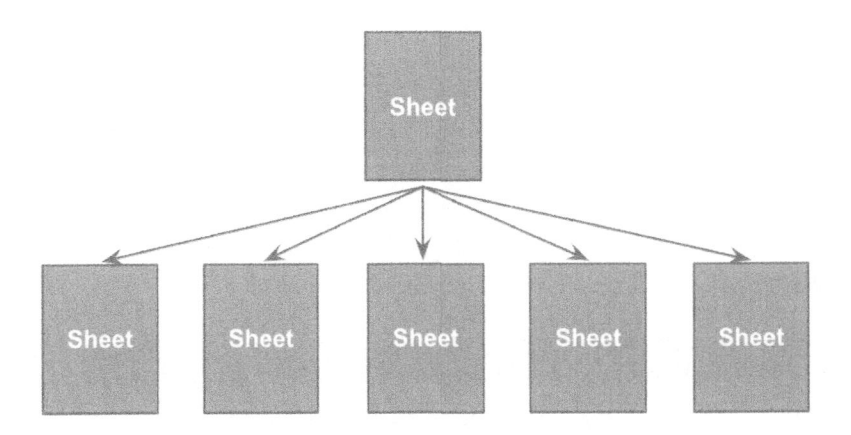

**Example 1 - How to use IMPORTRANGE**

Let's start with a simple example showing how you can connect different spreadsheets. I have a sheet, linked to a questionnaire form, where the responses from our student questionnaires are stored.

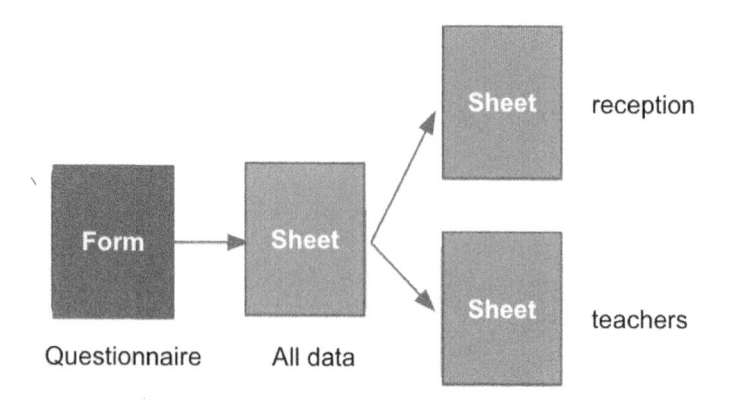

The students are asked questions about the teacher and also about the administration of their course and the service we provided during sign up, etc. I want to share the information about the admin process with reception but I don't want to show them the personal information about the teacher. So, what I can do is, create and share a sheet with reception and import the relevant information for them.

First, I create the sheet and share it with reception. Then in the *shared* file, in cell A1 I type the IMPORTRANGE function. You will see the useful help box appear.

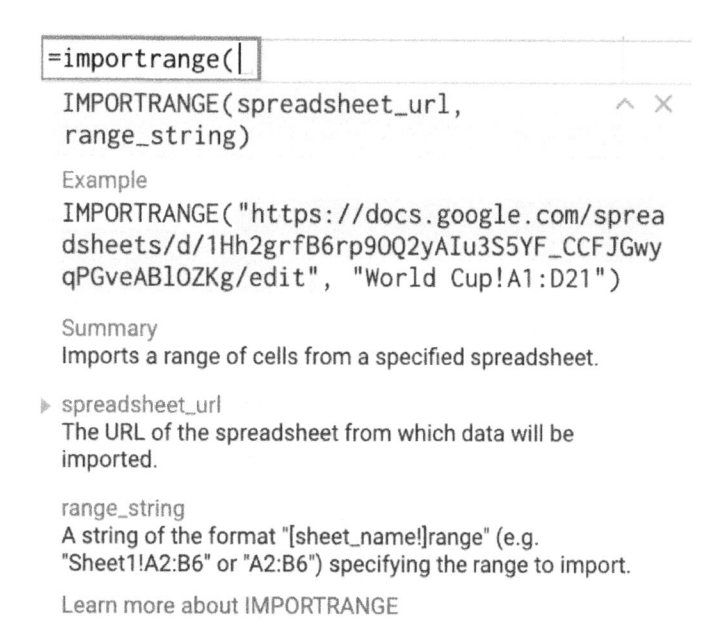

```
=importrange(
```

IMPORTRANGE(spreadsheet_url, range_string)

Example
IMPORTRANGE("https://docs.google.com/spreadsheets/d/1Hh2grfB6rp9OQ2yAIu3S5YF_CCFJGwyqPGveAB1OZKg/edit", "World Cup!A1:D21")

Summary
Imports a range of cells from a specified spreadsheet.

▸ spreadsheet_url
The URL of the spreadsheet from which data will be imported.

range_string
A string of the format "[sheet_name!]range" (e.g. "Sheet1!A2:B6" or "A2:B6") specifying the range to import.

Learn more about IMPORTRANGE

Get the spreadsheet URL from your browser:

https://docs.google.com/spreadsheets/d/11g7TliDDqU6Kfp2UMemEbWvam39SrjDZVzY6POXvZXY/edit

Copy this and then back on the shared file, add speech marks then paste the key in and add speech marks again. It won't work without the speech marks.

`=importrange("https://docs.google.com/spreadsheets/d/11g7TIiDDqU6Kfp2UMemEbWvam39SrjDZVzY6POXvZXY/edit"`

Now we need to tell it where the data we want is in that file. So, in our function, we first add the sheet name then the range. The sheet in this case is called "Questionnaire".

QUESTIONNAIRE ▾

So, we start with a comma after the URL we've just added, then speech marks again, then the name of the sheet followed by an exclamation mark, which tells Sheets this is a reference to a sheet.

Looking back at the original file, we can see we want the first 3 columns A to C and down to row 8. Columns D and E are about the course and the teacher.

|   | A | B | C |
|---|---|---|---|
| 1 | Questionnaire feedback | | |
| 2 | | ADMIN | |
| 3 | Date | How was the enrolment process? | How was the level test process? |
| 4 | 01/09/2016 | Very good | Excellent |
| 5 | 01/09/2016 | Very good | Excellent |
| 6 | 02/09/2016 | Poor | Very good |
| 7 | 02/09/2016 | Very good | Excellent |
| 8 | 03/09/2016 | Excellent | Excellent |

Finally, we add the range we want, A1:C8 and end with speech marks. then press Enter.

`,"QUESTIONNAIRE!A1:C8")`

The first time you try to link the sheet, the #REF! error will appear. Don't worry, it's just reminding you to do something.

Hover your mouse over the cell, and you'll see the box below appear asking you to "allow access". This is a security measure and is always necessary the first time you share the file. Just click the blue button to link the files.

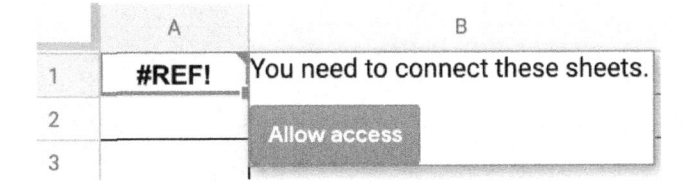

|   | A | B |
|---|---|---|
| 1 | #REF! | You need to connect these sheets. |
| 2 | | Allow access |
| 3 | | |

The contents of the range above will appear in the shared file. Note, that this only imports the content, i.e. the values of the cells, and not the formatting.

|   | A | B | C |
|---|---|---|---|
| 1 | **Questionnaire feedback** | | |
| 2 | | ADMIN | |
| 3 | Date | How was the enrolment process? | How was the level test process? |
| 4 | 01/09/2016 | Very good | Excellent |
| 5 | 01/09/2016 | Very good | Excellent |
| 6 | 02/09/2016 | Poor | Very good |
| 7 | 02/09/2016 | Very good | Excellent |
| 8 | 03/09/2016 | Excellent | Excellent |

So, sometimes you'll have to adjust the cells accordingly. More about that later.

And that's it! The two sheets are linked and if I make a change on the original sheet, it'll update the shared one automatically. Depending on the amount of information being imported, sometimes there is a slight delay in the second sheet updating. That's normal.

I of course do the same for the teachers and share just the ranges that apply to them.

**Example 2 - Open-ended ranges**

In the example above, we are only sharing a fixed range (A1:G8), but what happens if we receive some more questionnaire feedback and have data that is in rows 9 and above? The range we used above won't show us that data, so here we will need to use an **open-ended range**.

Let's slightly change our function at the end. Change the range from A1:C8 to **A:C**. As we don't state the row numbers, the range is in effect going from row 1 to infinity (well until the maximum number of rows).

```
,"QUESTIONNAIRE!A:C")
```

Here we've received two more pieces of feedback in row 9 and 10 in the original file.

|   | A | B | C | D | E |
|---|---|---|---|---|---|
| 1 | **Questionnaire feedback** | | | | |
| 2 | | ADMIN | | COURSE & TEACHER | |
| 3 | Date | How was the enrolment process? | How was the level test process? | How was the course? | How was the teacher? |
| 4 | 01/09/2016 | Very good | Excellent | Good | Good |
| 5 | 01/09/2016 | Very good | Excellent | Very good | Fair |
| 6 | 02/09/2016 | Poor | Very good | Poor | Poor |
| 7 | 02/09/2016 | Very good | Excellent | Good | Fair |
| 8 | 03/09/2016 | Excellent | Excellent | Good | Good |
| 9 | 05/09/2016 | Excellent | Excellent | Excellent | Excellent |
| 10 | 06/09/2016 | Excellent | Excellent | Excellent | Excellent |

And automatically it appears on the shared admin file, without having to update the range. Note, I added the shading at the bottom, just to highlight the new data added.

|   | A | B | C |
|---|---|---|---|
| 1 | **Questionnaire feedback** | | |
| 2 | | ADMIN | |
| 3 | Date | How was the enrolment process? | How was the level test process? |
| 4 | 01/09/2016 | Very good | Excellent |
| 5 | 01/09/2016 | Very good | Excellent |
| 6 | 02/09/2016 | Poor | Very good |
| 7 | 02/09/2016 | Very good | Excellent |
| 8 | 03/09/2016 | Excellent | Excellent |
| 9 | 05/09/2016 | Excellent | Excellent |
| 10 | 06/09/2016 | Excellent | Excellent |

**Example 3 - Multiple IMPORTRANGES on the same sheet**

So far, we've seen one range from one spreadsheet being imported into another spreadsheet. We're not limited to just one, if we wanted, we could import hundreds on the same sheet.

Let's look at another example where I have some details about two teachers on two different spreadsheets. They have access to their specific file and I want to combine this information in a master sheet, so the information for both teachers appears on one page.

First, we have the information in one file, on a page called Teacher 1.

|   | A | B |
|---|---|---|
| 1 | Name: | Alan Teacher |
| 2 | Address: | Calle San Pedro, 5. Seville |
| 3 | Phone no: | 6472872834 |
| 4 | Email address: | alan@teacher.com |
| 5 | Qualifications: | BA (Hons) English; DELTA |

Teacher 1 ▼

Second, we have the information about the other teacher in another file, on a page called Teacher 2.

|   | A | B |
|---|---|---|
| 1 | Name: | Ana Profe |
| 2 | Address: | Calle Santa Clara, 3. Seville |
| 3 | Phone no: | 6435894583 |
| 4 | Email address: | ana@profe.com |
| 5 | Qualifications: | MA English Literature |

Teacher 2 ▼

Each teacher only has access to their particular file to ensure privacy.

Now, I want to add them to a master sheet. In cell A1 I type in the first IMPORTRANGE function as below. So, exactly the same as above, I get the spreadsheet key of the first spreadsheet, then I refer to the 'Teacher 1' sheet and the range 'A1:B5'.

`=importrange("1mydHxuHOT0dLKsi3E2EtEzgSoDX3pnhdsu4t76PL0CA","Teacher 1!A1:B5")`

As always, I may need to tidy up the formatting, for example, here the column width and the alignment.

|   | A | B |
|---|---|---|
| 1 | Name: | Alan Teacher |
| 2 | Address: | Calle San Pedro, 5. Seville |
| 3 | Phone no: | 6472872834 |
| 4 | Email address: | alan@teacher.com |
| 5 | Qualifications: | BA (Hons) English; DELTA |

Now in cell C1, I add the second IMPORTRANGE function. I include the key from the second spreadsheet, refer to the page Teacher 2 and this time, I only need the column B.

`=importrange("1QnymEUSDYByUG0Bs2f0arjO0jMfU_aXXPpHvFOwmiWY","Teacher 2!B1:B5")`

I could continue adding teachers like this by adding another IMPORTRANGE function to D1, E1, etc.

|   | A | B | C |
|---|---|---|---|
| 1 | Name: | Alan Teacher | Ana Profe |
| 2 | Address: | Calle San Pedro, 5. Seville | Calle Santa Clara, 3. Seville |
| 3 | Phone no: | 6472872834 | 6435894583 |
| 4 | Email address: | alan@teacher.com | ana@profe.com |
| 5 | Qualifications: | BA (Hons) English; DELTA | MA English Literature |

If I'm expecting further information to be added, for example, qualifications to be updated, and therefore, extra rows added, I could of course use an open-ended range for each of the functions. For example, in the case of the first one the range would be **A:B** not A1:B5.

One important thing to note, is that you **cannot write anything within the imported range.** If you do, the data disappears and you get the #REF! error as you can see below (as we also saw with the FILTER function).

Here I typed the word "text" in cell C5 and that has caused the second teacher's details to disappear. so, you cannot edit the imported information, only the original data can be edited.

| B | C |
|---|---|
| Alan Teacher | #REF! |
| Calle San Pedro, 5. Seville | |
| 6472872834 | |
| alan@teacher.com | |
| BA (Hons) English; DELTA | text |

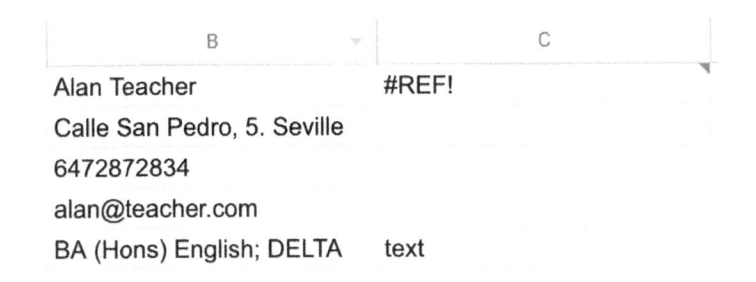

## Example 4 - Pre-formatting an imported range

In the above examples, we just had text and the imported range didn't look that good, and we had to format the cells afterwards. Let's look at how we can maintain the format of the original data in our new imported range.

Here I have the attendance for two classes (A & B) in two separate files and I want to add them into one file but with a tab for each class. This time the data is formatted in various ways, e.g. background colours, font size, bolding, conditional formatting, percentages, alignment. To reformat this for each imported class, would be a real pain. So, it's far better to set up the destination file with the same formatting, so when the data arrives, you don't need to do anything.

| | A | B | C | D | E | F | G |
|---|---|---|---|---|---|---|---|
| 1 | Class A Attendance | | | | | | |
| 2 | | Mon | Tue | Wed | Thu | Fri | Week |
| 3 | Fred | X | X | | X | X | 80% |
| 4 | Wilma | X | X | X | X | X | 100% |
| 5 | Barney | X | X | | | | 40% |
| 6 | Betty | X | X | | X | | 60% |

| | A | B | C | D | E | F | G |
|---|---|---|---|---|---|---|---|
| 1 | Class B Attendance | | | | | | |
| 2 | | Mon | Tue | Wed | Thu | Fri | Week |
| 3 | John | | | | X | X | 40% |
| 4 | Paul | X | | | X | | 40% |
| 5 | Ringo | | X | | | | 20% |
| 6 | George | X | X | | X | | 60% |

Here we're going to do two key things:

1. Use "Copy to..." to copy one of the original sheets to the destination one.
2. Use "duplicate" to create a copy of a blank formatted sheet.

First, from the Class A file, click on the sheet tab arrow and select "Copy to...".

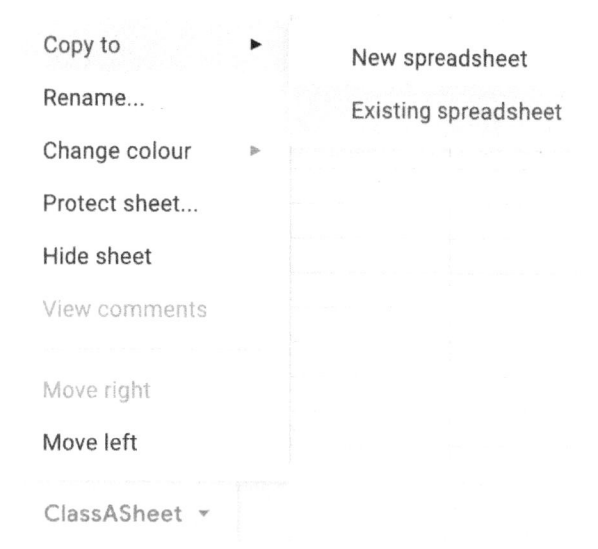

| | |
|---|---|
| Copy to ▶ | New spreadsheet |
| Rename... | Existing spreadsheet |
| Change colour ▶ | |
| Protect sheet... | |
| Hide sheet | |
| View comments | |
| Move right | |
| Move left | |
| ClassASheet ▾ | |

You then need to find and select the file you want to copy to. I often use click on "Recent" as usually the file I want has been worked on recently, so will appear near the top of the list.

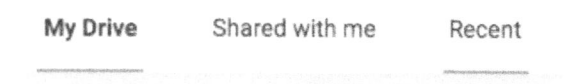

**My Drive**      Shared with me      Recent

Click on the file and click "Select".

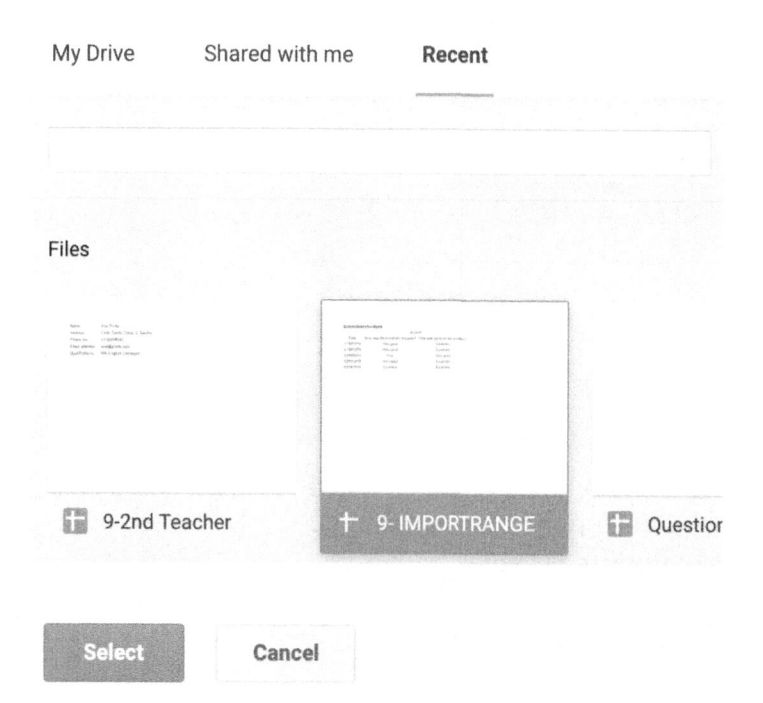

### Select a spreadsheet to copy this worksheet into

My Drive      Shared with me      **Recent**

Files

9-2nd Teacher      **9- IMPORTRANGE**      Question

[Select]   Cancel

You'll get a confirmation message and if you want to go to the destination file, click on "Open target workbook".

82                                                              9: IMPORTRANGE

**Sheet copied successfully**

Open spreadsheet

OK

Here it's added a new tab called "Copy of ClassASheet".

Copy of ClassASheet ▼

As you can see, it's identical to the original sheet.

|   | A | B | C | D | E | F | G |
|---|---|---|---|---|---|---|---|
| 1 | **Class A Attendance** | | | | | | |
| 2 |   | Mon | Tue | Wed | Thu | Fri | Week |
| 3 | Fred | X | X |   | X | X | 80% |
| 4 | Wilma | X | X | X | X | X | 100% |
| 5 | Barney | X | X |   |   |   | 40% |
| 6 | Betty | X | X |   | X |   | 60% |

Now select all the cells and press delete.

|   | A | B | C | D | E | F | G |
|---|---|---|---|---|---|---|---|
| 1 | **Class A Attendance** | | | | | | |
| 2 |   | Mon | Tue | Wed | Thu | Fri | Week |
| 3 | Fred | X | X |   | X | X | 80% |
| 4 | Wilma | X | X | X | X | X | 100% |
| 5 | Barney | X | X |   |   |   | 40% |
| 6 | Betty | X | X |   | X |   | 60% |

This will leave you with a pre-formatted blank.

|   | A | B | C | D | E | F | G |
|---|---|---|---|---|---|---|---|
| 1 |   |   |   |   |   |   |   |
| 2 |   |   |   |   |   |   |   |
| 3 |   |   |   |   |   |   |   |
| 4 |   |   |   |   |   |   |   |
| 5 |   |   |   |   |   |   |   |
| 6 |   |   |   |   |   |   |   |

Now as we have another class we want to import and I want to put it on a different sheet, click the sheet tab arrow and this time select "Duplicate". This will make a copy of the blank formatted sheet.

Duplicate

Copy to ▶

Rename...

Change colour ▶

Protect sheet...

Hide sheet

View comments

Move right

Move left

Copy of ClassASheet ▼

Now all we need to do is add our IMPORTRANGE functions. I add class A to the first sheet typing the function in cell A1 (although it could in fact be in any cell).

`=importrange("1mydHxuHOT0dLKsi3E2EtEzgSoDX3pnhdsu4t76PL0CA", "ClassASheet!A1:G6")`

As you can see it formats it perfectly automatically.

|   | A | B | C | D | E | F | G |
|---|---|---|---|---|---|---|---|
| 1 | **Class A Attendance** | | | | | | |
| 2 | | Mon | Tue | Wed | Thu | Fri | Week |
| 3 | Fred | X | X | | X | X | 80% |
| 4 | Wilma | X | X | X | X | X | 100% |
| 5 | Barney | X | X | | | | 40% |
| 6 | Betty | X | X | | X | | 60% |

Then I add class B.

`=importrange("1QnymEUSDYByUG0Bs2f0arjO0jMfU_aXXPpHvFOwmiWY","ClassBSheet!A1:G6")`

|   | A | B | C | D | E | F | G |
|---|---|---|---|---|---|---|---|
| 1 | **Class B Attendance** | | | | | | |
| 2 | | Mon | Tue | Wed | Thu | Fri | Week |
| 3 | John | | | | X | X | 40% |
| 4 | Paul | X | | | X | | 40% |
| 5 | Ringo | | X | | | | 20% |
| 6 | George | X | X | | X | | 60% |

So, now I have both class A and B in the same file, which saves me opening different files to see the information and to analyse the different sets of data in the same file. For example, I may want to produce a report for the attendance of all students and this can easily be done within the same file.

# 10: PROPER, UPPER, LOWER, TRIM

In this chapter, we're going to look at how we change the format of text to suit our needs, using the functions PROPER, UPPER, LOWER, and TRIM. It's particularly useful when working with text that has come from, for example, a form, a different computer system, or indeed someone has typed in on your Sheet. This is because the capitalisation isn't the way we want it and the text may contain unwanted spaces, which can cause problems on your Sheet. We'll cover the following areas:

- Using the PROPER function to capitalize each word
- Using the UPPER function to capitalize all letters
- Using the LOWER function to put words into lowercase
- Using the PROPER and TRIM functions to clean up text
- Using ARRAYFORMULA to copy PROPER function to all rows
- Capitalizing only the first letter of a sentence and putting the rest in lowercase
- Changing a name to initials

**Example 1 - Using the PROPER function to capitalize each word**

The PROPER function capitalizes every word in the text, which is useful for correcting the format of names. Here we've got my name in various formats.

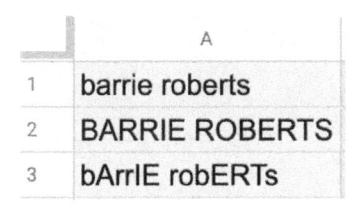

|   | A |
|---|---|
| 1 | barrie roberts |
| 2 | BARRIE ROBERTS |
| 3 | bArrIE robERTs |

As we can see the syntax of the PROPER function and indeed the UPPER, LOWER and TRIM functions is very simple, just add the text or cell reference in brackets.

```
=PROPER(
```

PROPER(text_to_capitalise)

Example
PROPER("google sheets")

Summary
Capitalises each word in a specified string.

▸ text_to_capitalise
The text which will be returned with the first letter of each word in upper case and all other letters in lower case.

Learn more about PROPER

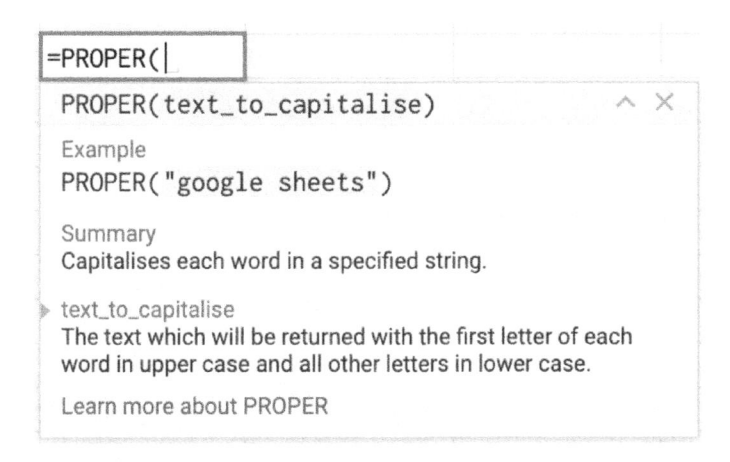

So, I write the following in cell A2.

=PROPER(A1)

Then I copy that down in cells B2 and B3, and as we can see it's corrected the format of the name.

| | A | B |
|---|---|---|
| 1 | barrie roberts | Barrie Roberts |
| 2 | BARRIE ROBERTS | Barrie Roberts |
| 3 | bArrIE robERTs | Barrie Roberts |

**Example 2 - Using the UPPER function to capitalize all letters**

Here we have a part number which should be in UPPERCASE.

| | A |
|---|---|
| 1 | fsdfDDFsd-101 |

Similar to PROPER you just put the text or cell reference in brackets.

=upper(A1)

And it changes all the letters to uppercase.

| | A | B |
|---|---|---|
| 1 | fsdfDDFsd-101 | FSDFDDFSD-101 |

**Example 3 - Using the LOWER function to put words into lowercase**

Here I want to change my messy name to lowercase.

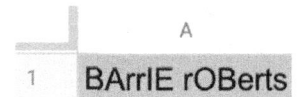

| | A |
|---|---|
| 1 | BArrIE rOBerts |

I just write the following function:

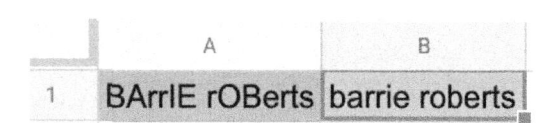

=lower(A1)

| | A | B |
|---|---|---|
| 1 | BArrIE rOBerts | barrie roberts |

## Example 4 - Using the PROPER and TRIM functions to clean up text

One problem with receiving text input from forms, computer systems, etc is that text input can be in different formats and also can have unwanted spaces, which can mess up your formulas and how you use the data.

Here is an example where my name has been filled out in a form, but the users have entered it in different ways.

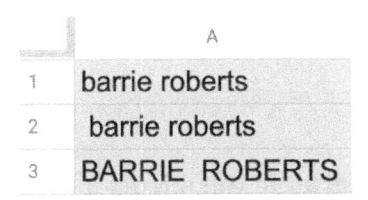

| | A |
|---|---|
| 1 | barrie roberts |
| 2 | barrie roberts |
| 3 | BARRIE  ROBERTS |

We can use the PROPER function to tidy up the format of the text, as we saw above, and we can use the TRIM function to get rid of those unwanted spaces, whether they are before the text, in the middle of the text, or afterwards.

So, we wrap the TRIM function up in the PROPER one:

```
=proper(trim(A1))
```

As you can see, it tidies it up well, making it easy to use the data afterwards, or even just to make it look better.

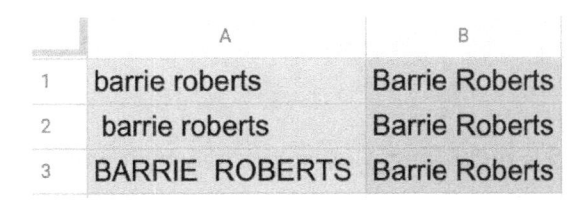

| | A | B |
|---|---|---|
| 1 | barrie roberts | Barrie Roberts |
| 2 | barrie roberts | Barrie Roberts |
| 3 | BARRIE  ROBERTS | Barrie Roberts |

## Example 5 - Using ARRAYFORMULA to copy PROPER function to all rows

In the example 1, I copied the PROPER function down into each row. There's a quicker and better way. Here I have some students' names and I want to tidy up the format.

| | A |
|---|---|
| 1 | paul mcCartney |
| 2 | JOHN LENNON |
| 3 | GeoRge harrison |
| 4 | ringo STARR |

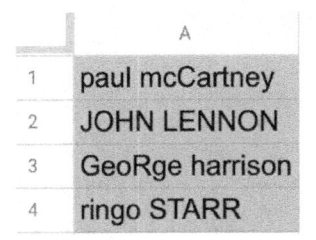

In cell B1, I write the following formula:

```
=arrayformula(proper(A1:A))
```

This looks at everything in column A and places the corrected format in column B, without having to copy down the formula into rows 2 and below.

|   | A | B |
|---|---|---|
| 1 | paul mcCartney | Paul Mccartney |
| 2 | JOHN LENNON | John Lennon |
| 3 | GeoRge harrison | George Harrison |
| 4 | ringo STARR | Ringo Starr |

Note, that when using the PROPER function, names which contain a capital letter in the middle of the word, such as, McCarthy, aren't displayed correctly, in that the second c is also in lowercase, e.g. Mccarthy.

**Example 6 - Capitalizing only the first letter of a sentence and putting the rest in lowercase**

The PROPER function works well with names, but what about normal sentences? We usually don't want every word to start with a capital letter.

Here, I have a sentence all in uppercase and as it seems that the person is 'shouting', I want to correct it automatically and add a capital letter at the start.

|   | A |
|---|---|
| 1 | THIS IS A SENTENCE WHERE WE ONLY WANT TO CAPITALIZE THE FIRST LETTER. |

This sounds like a simple thing to do, but the formula involved is quite long. However, the way it works is quite simple.

```
=UPPER(LEFT(A1,1))&LOWER(RIGHT(A1,LEN(A1)-1))
```

Let's go through it from left to right. Firstly, it puts the first character to the left in uppercase, i.e. the first letter of the sentence. Then it puts the rest of the sentence in lowercase, by finding out the length of the text and ignoring the 1 character at the start of the sentence.

Here's the result:

| A | B |
|---|---|
| THIS IS A SENTENCE WHERE WE ONLY WANT TO CAPITALIZE THE FIRST LETTER. | This is a sentence where we only want to capitalize the first letter. |

Here's the formula in case you want to copy and paste it into your sheet:

=UPPER(LEFT(A1,1))&LOWER(RIGHT(A1,LEN(A1)-1))

To adapt it to your needs, just edit the cell reference A1.

**Bonus Example - Changing a name to initials**

In Spain, names can be quite long as people can have two first names and also two surnames. A common practice in business, is to refer to people in emails and documents by their initials. We can get sheets to display the initials by looking at the full name and returned the first letter of each name.

| A |
|---|
| José María García Fernández |

This example is not strictly to do with the functions in this chapter, but is an example of how other functions can be used to manipulate names. The formula is particularly long, but in fact, from the second MID function, it just the same formula repeated to analyse each word in sequence.

```
=LEFT(A1)&MID(A1,FIND("#",SUBSTITUTE(A1&" "," ","#",1))+1,1)&MID(A1,FIND("#",SUBSTITUTE(A1&" "," ","#",2))+1,1)&MID(A1,FIND("#",SUBSTITUTE(A1&" "," ","#",3))+1,1)
```

As we can see it takes the four-word name and returns the person's initials.

| A | B |
|---|---|
| José María García Fernández | JMGF |

If the initial name was in lowercase, the initials would also be in lowercase.

With the formula split into 4 component parts, you can see that after the initial LEFT function, there are 3 parts that are almost identical. The only difference is that in the SUBSTITUTE formula, the number changes from 1 to 3.

=LEFT(A1)

&MID(A1,FIND("#",SUBSTITUTE(A1&" "," ","#",1))+1,1)

&MID(A1,FIND("#",SUBSTITUTE(A1&" "," ","#",2))+1,1)

&MID(A1,FIND("#",SUBSTITUTE(A1&" "," ","#",3))+1,1)

To adapt it to your needs, just edit the cell reference A1. If you only have 3 names, you can omit the last part. If you have more than 4 names, just add another &MID part, and make sure the number on the SUBSTITUTE brackets goes up by 1 (for example to 4).

# 11 - TRANSPOSE

In this chapter, we're going to look at how we can use the TRANSPOSE function to change our data from being vertical to being horizontal, or vice versa.

**Example 1 - Changing a single column or row of data**

Here we have the days of the week in a column and we want to put them horizontally, so that each day is in a different column across the page.

|   | A |
|---|---|
| 1 | Monday |
| 2 | Tuesday |
| 3 | Wednesday |
| 4 | Thursday |
| 5 | Friday |

In cell C1, I write the following function:

`=transpose(A1:A5)`

As you can see, it changes the information from being vertically stacked to being horizontally laid out.

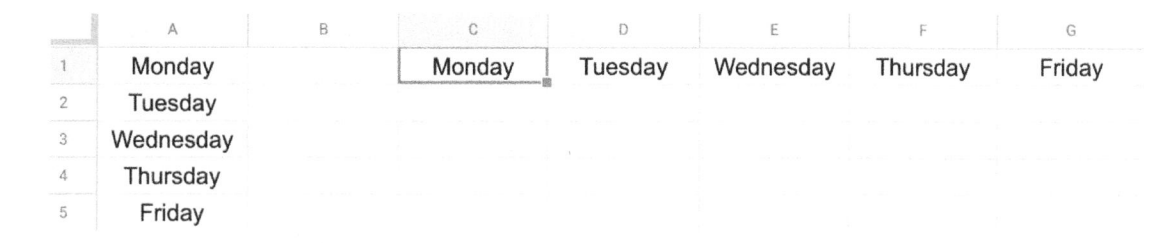

|   | A | B | C | D | E | F | G |
|---|---|---|---|---|---|---|---|
| 1 | Monday |  | Monday | Tuesday | Wednesday | Thursday | Friday |
| 2 | Tuesday |  |  |  |  |  |  |
| 3 | Wednesday |  |  |  |  |  |  |
| 4 | Thursday |  |  |  |  |  |  |
| 5 | Friday |  |  |  |  |  |  |

This works both ways. If the original data was horizontally laid out, then in cell A1, we could write this function:

`=TRANSPOSE(C1:G1)`

This would display the days vertically.

**Example 2 - Converting 2 vertical columns to 2 horizontal ones**

Here we have the days of the week and some teachers. I want to lay both sets of information horizontally.

|   | A | B |
|---|---|---|
| 1 | Monday | Fred |
| 2 | Tuesday | Wilma |
| 3 | Wednesday | Betty |
| 4 | Thursday | Barney |
| 5 | Friday | Baz |

This is easy, just include both columns in the range in the TRANSPOSE function.

`=transpose(A1:B5)`

This will then take column A and put it in row 1, then take column B and put it in row 2.

|   | A | B | C | D | E | F | G | H |
|---|---|---|---|---|---|---|---|---|
| 1 | Monday | Fred |   | Monday | Tuesday | Wednesday | Thursday | Friday |
| 2 | Tuesday | Wilma |   | Fred | Wilma | Betty | Barney | Baz |
| 3 | Wednesday | Betty |   |   |   |   |   |   |
| 4 | Thursday | Barney |   |   |   |   |   |   |
| 5 | Friday | Baz |   |   |   |   |   |   |

**Example 3 - Converting multiple horizontal rows into vertical columns**

Similar to the previous example, we can do the same for more than 2 sets of data.

|   | A | B | C |
|---|---|---|---|
| 1 | 1 | 2 | 3 |
| 2 | 4 | 5 | 6 |
| 3 | 7 | 8 | 9 |

Include the complete range in the TRANSPOSE function.

`=transpose(A1:C4)`

And sure enough, it transposes the information from rows to columns.

|   | A | B | C | D | E | F | G |
|---|---|---|---|---|---|---|---|
| 1 | 1 | 2 | 3 |   | 1 | 4 | 7 |
| 2 | 4 | 5 | 6 |   | 2 | 5 | 8 |
| 3 | 7 | 8 | 9 |   | 3 | 6 | 9 |

The above is using the TRANSPOSE function, to do it automatically for you, but remember you can also copy your data and using paste **transpose**, you can transpose it manually. Just right click, select Paste special, then Paste transpose.

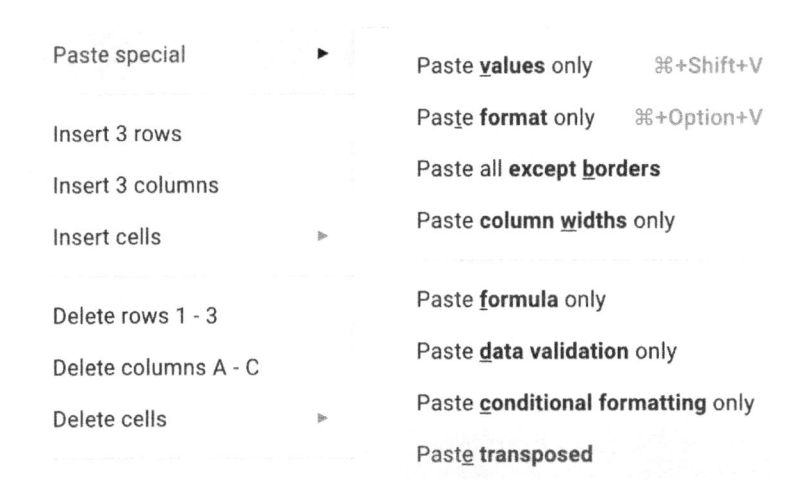

| | | | |
|---|---|---|---|
| Paste special | ▶ | Paste **values** only | ⌘+Shift+V |
| Insert 3 rows | | Pas**t**e **format** only | ⌘+Option+V |
| Insert 3 columns | | Paste all **except borders** | |
| Insert cells | ▶ | Paste **column widths** only | |
| | | | |
| Delete rows 1 - 3 | | Paste **formula** only | |
| Delete columns A - C | | Paste **data validation** only | |
| Delete cells | ▶ | Paste **conditional formatting** only | |
| | | Pas**t**e **transposed** | |

# 12: ISEMAIL, ISNUMBER, ISURL, NOT

In this chapter, we'll look at how we can check that emails addresses are in the correct format, that numbers are indeed numbers, and that website addresses (URLs) are in the correct format. We'll start with the basic checking of these and then move on to how we can highlight these using conditional formatting.

Throughout this chapter, we're going to use the information in the table below. Here we have information relating to some parents of children at the school. We have their email address, phone numbers and the website where they can access their child's reports.
We wish to check that their email, phone number and website URL are in formats that can be used.

|   | A | B | C | D | E | F | G |
|---|---|---|---|---|---|---|---|
| 1 | Parent | Email | Phone | Website URL | Email OK? | Number? | URL ok? |
| 2 | John Smith | john.smith@gmail.com | 123345243 | www.schoolreports.com/JS | TRUE | TRUE | TRUE |
| 3 | George Harris | georgeharris@hotmail.com | 23423-4566 | schoolreports.com/GH | TRUE | FALSE | TRUE |
| 4 | Maria Forward | mf123@yahoo.co.uk | 123 345 567 | schoolreports/MF | TRUE | FALSE | FALSE |
| 5 | Natasha Walsh | nat-walabcd.com | 0099854345345 | www.schoolreports.comm/NW | FALSE | FALSE | FALSE |
| 6 | Ian Arrowsmith | ianarrowsmith@hotmail.c | 123-PHONE-ME | schoolreports.com\IA | FALSE | FALSE | FALSE |

**Example 1 - Checking email addresses**

In column B, we have their email addresses (obviously fictitious ones).

| B |
|---|
| Email |
| john.smith@gmail.com |
| georgeharris@hotmail.com |
| mf123@yahoo.co.uk |
| nat-walabcd.com |
| ianarrowsmith@hotmail.c |

To check to see if the format of these email addresses is ok, in column E we write the following function:

`=ISEMAIL(B2)`

This checks that the contents of cell B2 is in fact an email address. If it is, it returns the word "TRUE". If not, it returns the word "FALSE". We then copy that formula down the rows B3 to B6.

As we can see, it correctly identified that there is a problem with the last two addresses. We can see that the fourth one is missing the @ symbol and the fifth one is missing something like .com, or .co.uk at the end.

| Email OK? |
|---|
| TRUE |
| TRUE |
| TRUE |
| FALSE |
| FALSE |

**Example 2 - Checking for numbers**

This time we want to check that the phone numbers in column C, are numbers and are not text or contain characters that maybe the computer system can't handle.

| Phone |
|---|
| 123345243 |
| 23423-4566 |
| 123 345 567 |
| 0099854345345 |
| 123-PHONE-ME |

To do this we write the following function:

=ISNUMBER(C2)

This time it looks at cell C2 and checks to see it's a number. If it is a number it returns "TRUE" and if not, it returns "FALSE".

As we can see it's found lots of problems. In cell C3, the number has a dash. In cell C4 there are spaces between the numbers. In cell C6, it's obviously got some letters in there.

| Number? |
|---|
| TRUE |
| FALSE |
| FALSE |
| FALSE |
| FALSE |

In cell C5, this number was entered as text and not a number, as it has a single apostrophe before the number to allow the number to start with a zero.

'0099854345345

All of these situations mean that the contents of those cells aren't numbers, at least in the way Sheets sees them.

### Example 3 - Checking website addresses (URLs)

This time we want to check that the URLs in column D are in the correct format.

| D |
| --- |
| **Website URL** |
| www.schoolreports.com/JS |
| schoolreports.com/GH |
| schoolreports/MF |
| www.schoolreports.comm/NW |
| schoolreports.com\IA |

We write this function in cell G2:

=ISURL(D2)

This checks to see that the URL in cell D2 is ok.

As we can see, the first two are ok, but the last three have problems. In cell D4, the URL is missing the .com (or similar). In cell D5, the .com has 2 'm's. In cell D6, the backslash is a forward slash.

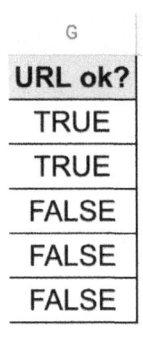

| G |
| --- |
| **URL ok?** |
| TRUE |
| TRUE |
| FALSE |
| FALSE |
| FALSE |

Note, that the URLs don't need the http: part nor the www. part to be recognised as genuine URLs. Sheets also automatically highlights correct URLs as hyperlinks.

### Example 4 - Displaying different text depending on whether it's TRUE or FALSE

In the examples above, our functions were displaying either TRUE or FALSE, which fine for a quick check, but don't really look that good on your sheet. In the next few example, we'll look at how we can improve that feedback.

Firstly, we can change the wording from TRUE and FALSE to anything we would like. For example, let's report 'OK' if it comes back TRUE if it's an email, and 'Not OK' if it's not.

|   | A | B | C | D | E | F | G |
|---|---|---|---|---|---|---|---|
| 1 | Parent | Email | Phone | Website URL | Email OK? | Number? | URL ok? |
| 2 | John Smith | john.smith@gmail.com | 123345243 | www.schoolreports.com/JS | OK | OK | OK |
| 3 | George Harris | georgeharris@hotmail.com | 23423-4566 | schoolreports.com/GH | OK | Not OK | OK |
| 4 | Maria Forward | mf123@yahoo.co.uk | 123 345 567 | schoolreports/MF | OK | Not OK | Not OK |
| 5 | Natasha Walsh | nat-walabcd.com | 0099854345345 | www.schoolreports.comm/NW | Not OK | Not OK | Not OK |
| 6 | Ian Arrowsmith | ianarrowsmith@hotmail.c | 123-PHONE-ME | schoolreports.com\IA | Not OK | Not OK | Not OK |

In column E, we write the following formula:

```
=if(ISEMAIL(B2),"OK", "Not OK")
```

This wraps the ISEMAIL function in an IF function. It looks at the content of cell B2 and if it's true, it displays 'OK' and if it's false it displays 'Not OK'.

Then we do the same for the other functions:

```
=if(ISNUMBER(C2), "OK", "Not OK")
```

```
=if(ISURL(D2), "OK", "Not OK")
```

Now in columns E to G, we can see which ones are OK and which ones aren't. This makes it a little clearer to anyone looking at your sheet.

| E | F | G |
|---|---|---|
| Email OK? | Number? | URL ok? |
| OK | OK | OK |
| OK | Not OK | OK |
| OK | Not OK | Not OK |
| Not OK | Not OK | Not OK |
| Not OK | Not OK | Not OK |

**Example 5 - Adding conditional formatting**

Now let's add some colour to show which are OK and not OK more clearly. Let's put the OKs in green and the Not OKs in red.

| | A | B | C | D | E | F | G |
|---|---|---|---|---|---|---|---|
| 1 | Parent | Email | Phone | Website URL | Email OK? | Number? | URL ok? |
| 2 | John Smith | john.smith@gmail.com | 123345243 | www.schoolreports.com/JS | OK | OK | OK |
| 3 | George Harris | georgeharris@hotmail.com | 23423-4566 | schoolreports.com/GH | OK | Not OK | OK |
| 4 | Maria Forward | mf123@yahoo.co.uk | 123 345 567 | schoolreports/MF | OK | Not OK | Not OK |
| 5 | Natasha Walsh | nat-walabcd.com | 0099854345345 | www.schoolreports.comm/NW | Not OK | Not OK | Not OK |
| 6 | Ian Arrowsmith | ianarrowsmith@hotmail.c | 123-PHONE-ME | schoolreports.com\IA | Not OK | Not OK | Not OK |

Select the cells you want to colour.

| E | F | G |
|---|---|---|
| Email OK? | Number? | URL ok? |
| OK | OK | OK |
| OK | Not OK | OK |
| OK | Not OK | Not OK |
| Not OK | Not OK | Not OK |
| Not OK | Not OK | Not OK |

Right click and select Conditional formatting.

> Insert note
>
> Conditional formatting...
>
> Data validation...

This opens the Conditional format rules sidebar. Click on where it says "Cell is not empty".

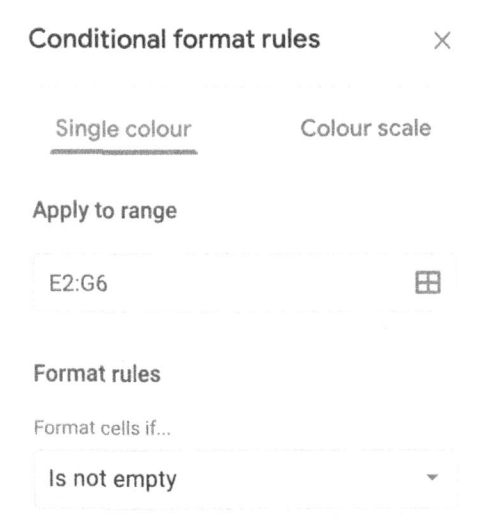

**Conditional format rules**    ✕

Single colour    Colour scale

Apply to range

E2:G6

**Format rules**

Format cells if...

Is not empty ▾

Then select "Is equal to" from the options.

98                    12: ISEMAIL, ISNUMBER, ISURL, NOT

Less than

Less than or equal to

Is equal to

Is not equal to

In the box type "OK".

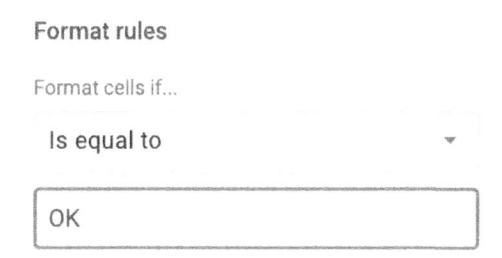

**Format rules**

Format cells if...

Is equal to ▼

OK

Then select the colour you want by clicking on the fill icon. As we can see, the first rule is now set up and it'll fill any cell in with green that is equal to OK.

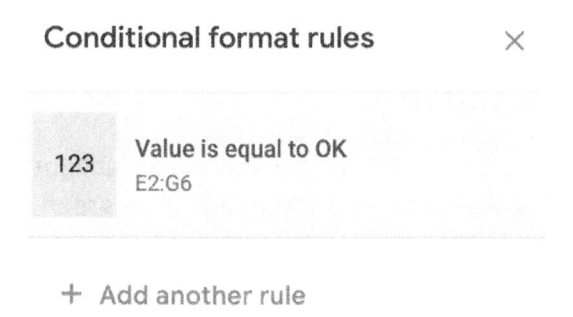

**Conditional format rules** ✕

123  Value is equal to OK
     E2:G6

＋ Add another rule

Click on "Add new rule". Then repeat the process above, this time selecting red and, in the box, typing in Not OK.

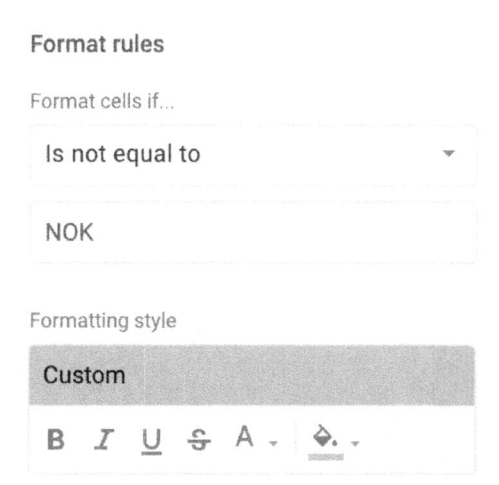

**Format rules**

Format cells if...

Is not equal to ▼

NOK

Formatting style

Custom

B  *I*  U  S  A ▾  ◇ ▾

99                                    12: ISEMAIL, ISNUMBER, ISURL, NOT

## Conditional format rules ×

**123** Value is equal to OK
E2:G6

**123** Value is not equal to NOK
E2:G6

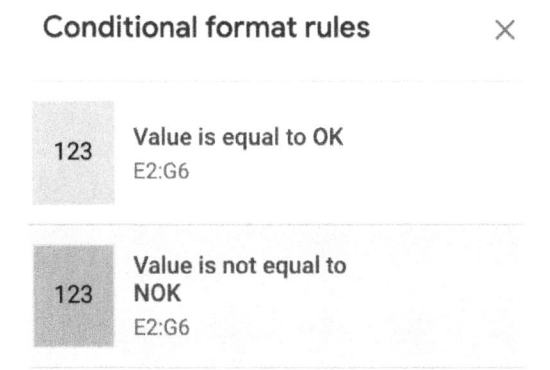

This is far more visual and effective, especially if you have a long list.

| Email OK? | Number? | URL ok? |
|---|---|---|
| OK | OK | OK |
| OK | Not OK | OK |
| OK | Not OK | Not OK |
| Not OK | Not OK | Not OK |
| Not OK | Not OK | Not OK |

**Example 6 - Using custom formula to add colour to cells with the data in it**

So far, we've reported what's OK and not OK in different cells, but often the better way is to highlight the cells themselves that are OK or not OK. For example, let's highlight the emails that are OK in green.

| | A | B |
|---|---|---|
| 1 | Parent | Email |
| 2 | John Smith | john.smith@gmail.com |
| 3 | George Harris | georgeharris@hotmail.com |
| 4 | Maria Forward | mf123@yahoo.co.uk |
| 5 | Natasha Walsh | nat-walabcd.com |
| 6 | Ian Arrowsmith | ianarrowsmith@hotmail.c |

Select the emails and right-click and select Conditional formatting as before.

| B |
|---|
| Email |
| john.smith@gmail.com |
| georgeharris@hotmail.com |
| mf123@yahoo.co.uk |
| nat-walabcd.com |
| ianarrowsmith@hotmail.c |

This time, at the bottom of the options, select "Custom formula is".

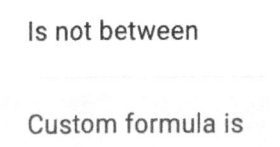

- Is not between
- Custom formula is

In the box, type the ISEMAIL function referring to the first cell in your selection. In this case, cell B2.

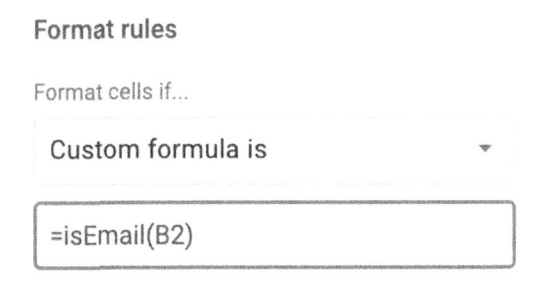

**Format rules**

Format cells if...

Custom formula is ▼

=isEmail(B2)

Note that this automatically, applies your formula to the whole range you selected.

**Apply to range**

B2:B6

As we can see it highlights those emails that are indeed emails, i.e. which from the formula return as true.

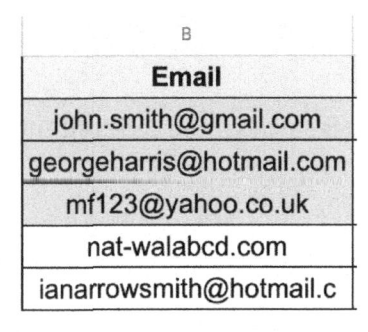

| B |
|---|
| **Email** |
| john.smith@gmail.com |
| georgeharris@hotmail.com |
| mf123@yahoo.co.uk |
| nat-walabcd.com |
| ianarrowsmith@hotmail.c |

## Example 7 - Using NOT in a custom formula to highlight what isn't true

Highlighting which emails are correct is fine, but I usually find that you normally want to know where there are any problem ones, as one assumes that the majority will be ok. As you can see in the picture below, we can clearly see which cells need attention.

| | A | B | C | D |
|---|---|---|---|---|
| 1 | Parent | Email | Phone | Website URL |
| 2 | John Smith | john.smith@gmail.com | 123345243 | www.schoolreports.com/JS |
| 3 | George Harris | georgeharris@hotmail.com | 23423-4566 | schoolreports.com/GH |
| 4 | Maria Forward | mf123@yahoo.co.uk | 123 345 567 | schoolreports/MF |
| 5 | Natasha Walsh | nat-walabcd.com | 0099854345345 | www.schoolreports.comm/NW |
| 6 | Ian Arrowsmith | ianarrowsmith@hotmail.c | 123-PHONE-ME | schoolreports.com\IA |

The process is exactly the same as the previous example, except we're going to change the formula slightly. Start off with the emails.

| B |
|---|
| **Email** |
| john.smith@gmail.com |
| georgeharris@hotmail.com |
| mf123@yahoo.co.uk |
| nat-walabcd.com |
| ianarrowsmith@hotmail.c |

Having selected "Custom formula is", type the following formula in the box:

**Format rules**

Format cells if...

Custom formula is

=NOT(isemail(B2))

This wraps the ISEMAIL function in a NOT function. Effectively, what it's doing is saying if the cell content ISN'T an email, then apply the formatting. We then add a red fill.

As we can see it's highlighted the problematic cells in red.

| B |
|---|
| **Email** |
| john.smith@gmail.com |
| georgeharris@hotmail.com |
| mf123@yahoo.co.uk |
| nat-walabcd.com |
| ianarrowsmith@hotmail.c |

We can then do the same for the numbers and URLs, selecting each range at a time and entering the following formulas.

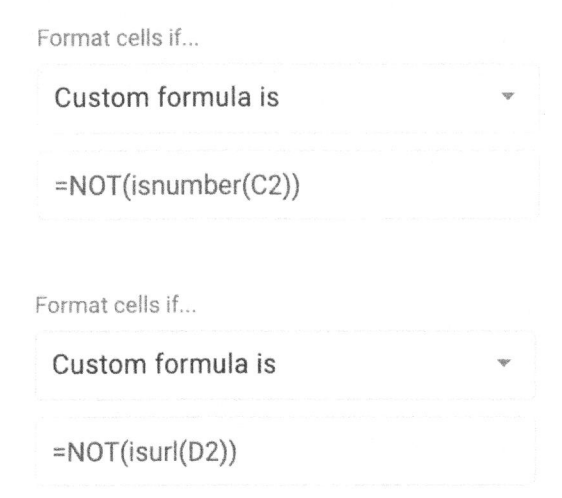

Format cells if...

| Custom formula is ▼ |
|---|

| =NOT(isnumber(C2)) |
|---|

Format cells if...

| Custom formula is ▼ |
|---|

| =NOT(isurl(D2)) |
|---|

This is much clearer and without the need of extra columns.

|   | A | B | C | D |
|---|---|---|---|---|
| 1 | **Parent** | **Email** | **Phone** | **Website URL** |
| 2 | John Smith | john.smith@gmail.com | 123345243 | www.schoolreports.com/JS |
| 3 | George Harris | georgeharris@hotmail.com | 23423-4566 | schoolreports.com/GH |
| 4 | Maria Forward | mf123@yahoo.co.uk | 123 345 567 | schoolreports/MF |
| 5 | Natasha Walsh | nat-walabcd.com | 0099854345345 | www.schoolreports.comm/NW |
| 6 | Ian Arrowsmith | ianarrowsmith@hotmail.c | 123-PHONE-ME | schoolreports.com\IA |

# 13: UNIQUE, COUNTUNIQUE, SORT

In this chapter, we'll look at how we can remove duplicates from a set of data, with one simple formula using the UNIQUE function. We'll also use the SORT function to put the unique list in order and use this in a drop-down menu using DATA VALIDATION. Finally, we'll look at counting those entries by using COUNTUNIQUE.

So, in detail we´ll look at:

- Using the UNIQUE function to list unique occurrences in a list
- Using UNIQUE with SORT to sort the unique list
- Making a drop-down menu from a list
- Making an alphabetical drop-down menu from a list
- Using COUNTUNIQUE to count how many things you have in the list, whilst ignoring duplicates
- Using UNIQUE to look for unique occurrences with 2 or more criteria

Let's use a list of books as an example. Here I've got a list of the copies of books we have. In reality this is over 2,000 books, but we have multiple copies of most of the books.

| | A |
|---|---|
| 1 | Books |
| 2 | Trinity GESE Grades 3-4 |
| 3 | Trinity GESE Grades 1-2 |
| 4 | English File (3rd Edition) |
| 5 | English File (3rd Edition) |
| 6 | Business Result |
| 7 | Market Leader (3rd Edition) |
| 8 | Business Result |
| 9 | Business Result |
| 10 | English File (3rd Edition) |
| 11 | Business Benchmark |
| 12 | Business Benchmark |
| 13 | Travel and Tourism - Standard level |
| 14 | Straightforward |
| 15 | Straightforward |
| 16 | Objective Advanced |

**Example 1 - Using the UNIQUE function to list unique occurrences in a list**

I want a list of what books we have without having the duplicates included in it. In a spare cell, I write the following formula:

=unique(A2:A16)

This looks at the list of books and returns 1 instance of each one. In this example, we have 9 different books.

| C |
|---|
| Trinity GESE Grades 3-4 |
| Trinity GESE Grades 1-2 |
| English File (3rd Edition) |
| Business Result |
| Market Leader (3rd Edition) |
| Business Benchmark |
| Travel and Tourism - Standard level |
| Straightforward |
| Objective Advanced |

**Example 2 - Using UNIQUE with SORT to sort the unique list**

I can also sort the above list into alphabetical order by wrapping the unique function up in a SORT function. I write the following formula:

```
=sort(unique(A2:A16),1,TRUE)
```

The SORT function contains three parts:

range, column to sort (number), is it to be sorted in ascending order

So, we put the UNIQUE function in the range part, then tell it's column 1 (in fact there is only one column), and we put TRUE in the final part to sort it in ascending order, i.e. A to Z.

Here we have the list sorted.

| E |
|---|
| Business Benchmark |
| Business Result |
| English File (3rd Edition) |
| Market Leader (3rd Edition) |
| Objective Advanced |
| Straightforward |
| Travel and Tourism - Standard level |
| Trinity GESE Grades 1-2 |
| Trinity GESE Grades 3-4 |

**Example 3 - Making a drop-down menu from a list**

One reason why I often do this, is that I use this list in a drop-down menu. So, when I add books to the list, I don't have to type in the full names every time, I just select the book I want from the list.

To create a drop-down list, you need to add 'Data validation' to the cell. It's sounds awfully technical, but really it just means it limits what you can write in the cell, and in this case, it will expect a book name from the list.

Right-click on a spare cell, then select "Data validation" from the bottom of the list.

Insert note

Conditional formatting...

Data validation...

This takes you to the Data validation dialogue box. The main part to use is the box to the right of where it says "List from a range". Click the little grid in the box.

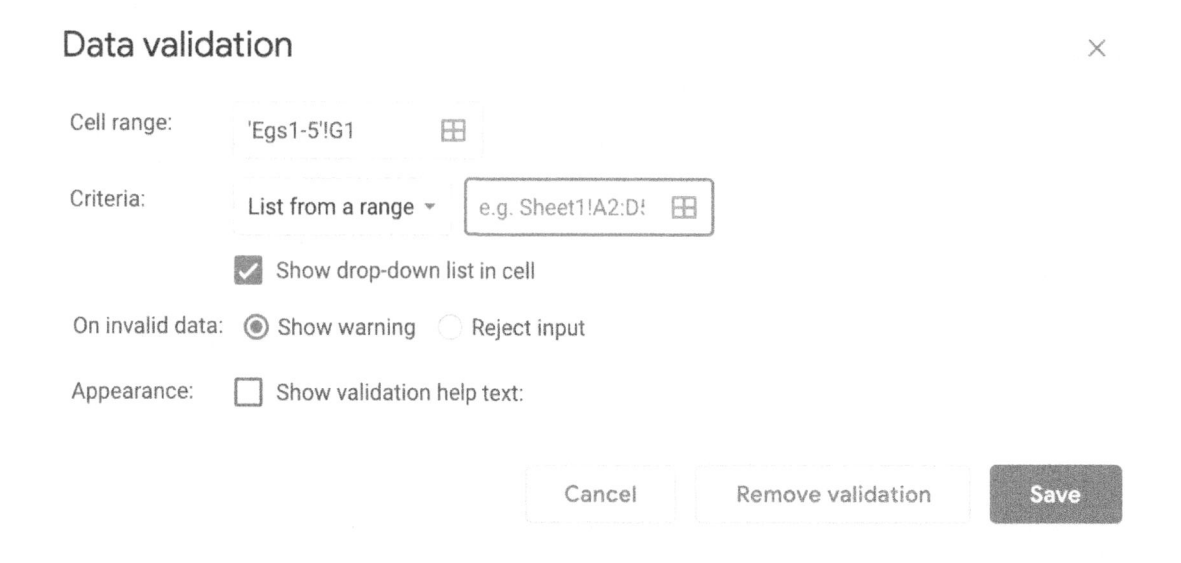

Data validation                                                     ×

Cell range:        'Egs1-5'!G1

Criteria:          List from a range ▼    e.g. Sheet1!A2:D!

                   ☑ Show drop-down list in cell

On invalid data:   ● Show warning    ○ Reject input

Appearance:        ☐ Show validation help text:

                                    Cancel    Remove validation    **Save**

This asks you to add the range you want. You can either type it in or just select the cells you want and the range gets added automatically. Click OK.

Select a data range                    ×

A2:A16

                   Cancel    **OK**

106                                          13: UNIQUE, COUNTUNIQUE, SORT

This has added the range of books, now click OK.

## Data validation

Cell range: 'Egs1-5'!F1

Criteria: List from a range ▼ A2:A16

☑ Show drop-down list in cell

On invalid data: ● Show warning  ○ Reject input

Appearance: ☐ Show validation help text:

Cancel    Remove validation    **Save**

In the cell, you will now see a little inverted triangle. This is the drop-down menu symbol.

Clicking on the triangle will open the drop-down menu and your list of books. Note, that as I've used the original list of books, this has automatically made a unique list of the books, i.e. there are no duplicates. The only thing is, is that it isn't sorted alphabetically, just in the order the books first appeared in the original list.

- Trinity GESE Grades 3-4
- Trinity GESE Grades 1-2
- English File (3rd Edition)
- Business Result
- Market Leader (3rd Edition)
- Business Benchmark
- Travel and Tourism - Standard level
- Straightforward
- Objective Advanced

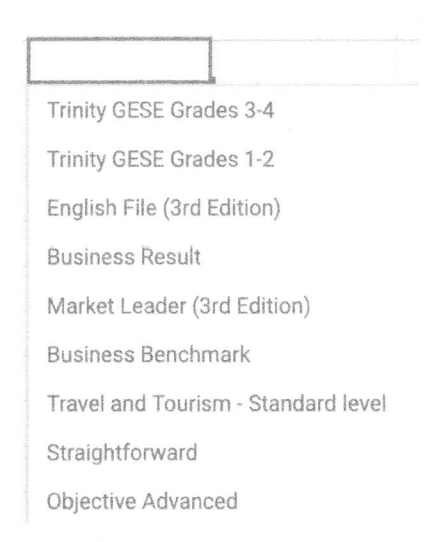

## Example 4 - Making an alphabetical drop-down menu from a list

This is where our sorted list comes in. I right-click on a spare cell and select Data validation as before. This time I enter the range where the sorted unique book list is, in this case in cells E2 to E17. Click OK.

List from a range ▼    'Egs1-5'!E2:E17

This time, clicking on the triangle, opens the same list but this time sorted alphabetically, which is much more useful and easier to use.

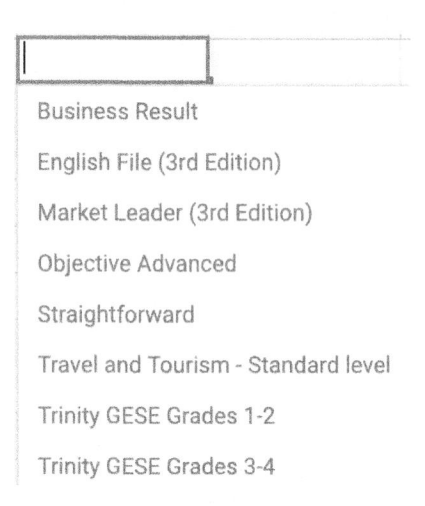

- Business Result
- English File (3rd Edition)
- Market Leader (3rd Edition)
- Objective Advanced
- Straightforward
- Travel and Tourism - Standard level
- Trinity GESE Grades 1-2
- Trinity GESE Grades 3-4

## Example 5 - Using COUNTUNIQUE to count how many things you have in the list, whilst ignoring duplicates

This time I want to know how many different books I have in the original list. I write the following formula:

`=COUNTUNIQUE(A2:A16)`

As you can see, it's correctly identified that there are in fact 9 different books.

9

## Example 6 - Using UNIQUE to look for unique occurrences with 2 or more criteria

All the examples above looked at a single column. UNIQUE can in fact look across multiple columns. In our book example, I've just looked at the name of the book, but in fact these books come in different levels and quite often I need to know how many of a specific book and level we have, to make sure there are enough copies for all the teachers.

Here's the list I'm going to use. It has the book title and the level of the book.

| | A | B |
|---|---|---|
| 1 | **Book** | **Level** |
| 2 | English File | Intermediate |
| 3 | English File | Intermediate |
| 4 | Business Result | Pre-Intermediate |
| 5 | Market Leader | Pre-Intermediate |
| 6 | Business Result | Advanced |
| 7 | Business Result | Intermediate |
| 8 | English File | Elementary |
| 9 | English File | Pre-Intermediate |
| 10 | English File | Elementary |
| 11 | Business Result | Advanced |
| 12 | Market Leader | Pre-Intermediate |

In cell D2 I write the following formula:

```
=sort(unique(A2:B15),1, TRUE)
```

This is the same formula as example 2, except that the range now includes column B. This finds unique occurrences where both column A and B together are unique. Therefore, it includes 3 examples of the book "Business Result", but each one is a different level.

| D | E |
|---|---|
| **Book** | **Level** |
| Business Result | Pre-Intermediate |
| Business Result | Advanced |
| Business Result | Intermediate |
| English File | Intermediate |
| English File | Elementary |
| English File | Pre-Intermediate |
| Market Leader | Pre-Intermediate |

If we want an alphabetical list, then we modify the formula, to add a second sort column:

```
=sort(unique(A2:B15),1, TRUE,2,TRUE)
```

This sort column 1 alphabetically A to Z, then column 2 A to Z.

| Book | Level |
|---|---|
| Business Result | Advanced |
| Business Result | Intermediate |
| Business Result | Pre-Intermediate |
| English File | Elementary |
| English File | Intermediate |
| English File | Pre-Intermediate |
| Market Leader | Pre-Intermediate |

One final thing I often do is, to include a range which is longer than the current range or an open-ended range. This means that if I add some new books in the original list, they will automatically be seen by the UNIQUE function, rather than have to edit the range every time a book is added. This is because UNIQUE ignores spaces.

So, the formula would be something like this:

```
=sort(unique(A2:B),1, TRUE)
```

Note, that column B has no number as it's looking at the whole of column B, so if anything is added into that column or in fact column A, it will automatically be included in the search range of the unique list.

# 14: NOW, TODAY, DAY, MONTH, YEAR, HOUR, MINUTE, SECOND

In this chapter, we're going to look at some of the basic date functions and in particular, how we can extract parts of a date or a time. We'll cover: NOW, TODAY, DAY, MONTH, YEAR, HOUR, MINUTE, and SECOND.

**Example 1 - Getting the current date and time**

We can add the current date and time to our sheet with the very simple function, NOW.

Type the following:

```
=NOW()
```

This will add the current date and time in the cell.

|   | A |
|---|---|
| 1 | 26/05/2019 19:04:55 |

This doesn't update every second, but by default will update every time there's a change made on the sheet. We can alter this by changing the recalculation settings. Go to "File" then "Spreadsheet settings".

Document details...

Spreadsheet settings...

Print ⌘P

## Settings for this spreadsheet

**General** | Calculation

**Locale**

United Kingdom ▾ — This affects formatting details such as functions, dates and currency.

**Time zone**

(GMT+01:00) Madrid ▾ — Your spreadsheet's history will be recorded in this time zone. This will change all time-related functions.

Display language: English (United Kingdom)

Cancel | **Save settings**

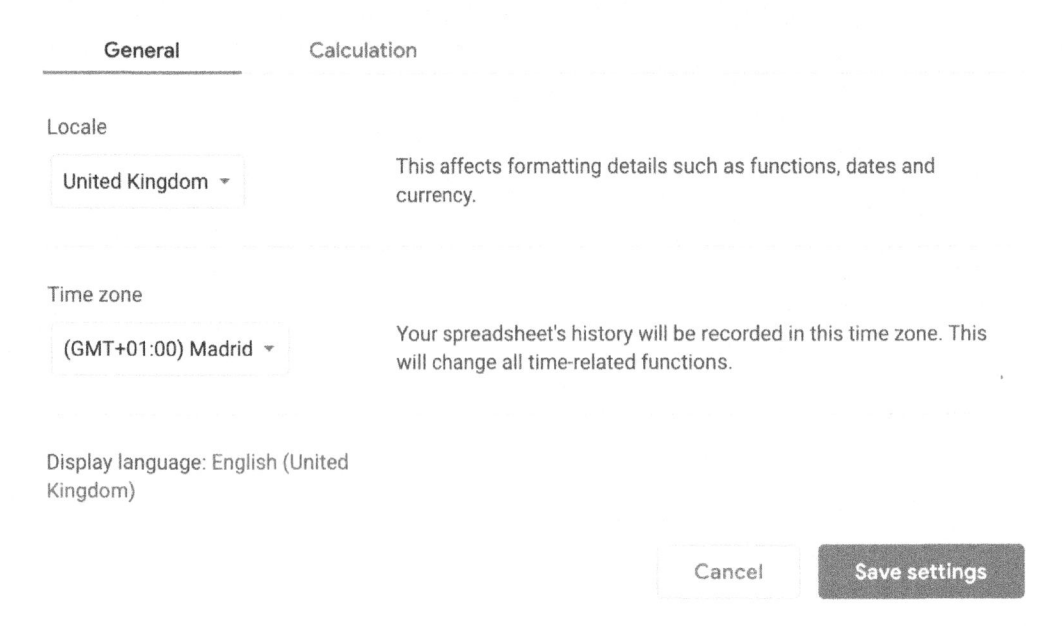

Under "Calculation", click the drop-down menu that says "On change".

## Settings for this spreadsheet

General | **Calculation**

**Recalculation**

On change ▾ — This affe updated.

Here you will have three options. Choose the one you want, then click "Save settings".

**Recalculation**

- On change
- On change and every minute
- On change and every hour

### Example 2 - Getting today's date and using it in calculations

Similar to above, we can get today's date by using the TODAY function. Type the following:

=TODAY()

This adds today's date in the cell.

|   | A |
|---|---|
| 1 | 26/05/2019 |

We often use this function in calculations. For example, let's find out how many days are left until Christmas day.

In cell B1 I have Christmas day and in cell C1 I type the following:

```
=B1-today()
```

This just subtracts Christmas day from today's date and returns the number of days, which at the time of writing, there are 213.

|   | A | B | C |
|---|---|---|---|
| 1 | 26/05/2019 | 25/12/2019 | 213 |

We can improve the returned result by adding some text to show what it is.

We start with the same formula as before, then add an ampersand and within inverted commas, we add the text we want.

```
=B1-today()&" days to Christmas"
```

As we can see, this adds the number of days to the text. This will count down every day.

| D |
|---|
| 213 days to Christmas |

**Example 3 - Extracting the day from a date**

Sometimes we want to extract a particular part of the date, to find out some piece of information. As an example, here we have the number of students that signed up for courses. The courses start either on 1st of the month, or on 15th. The Marketing department want to know which is more popular, the 1st or the 15th. From the data, it's difficult to see.

| | A | B |
|---|---|---|
| 1 | | Num of students |
| 2 | 01/10/2016 | 50 |
| 3 | 15/10/2016 | 80 |
| 4 | 01/11/2016 | 80 |
| 5 | 15/11/2016 | 90 |
| 6 | 01/12/2016 | 100 |
| 7 | 15/12/2016 | 50 |
| 8 | 01/01/2016 | 40 |
| 9 | 15/12/2016 | 80 |
| 10 | 01/02/2017 | 50 |
| 11 | 15/02/2017 | 80 |
| 12 | 01/03/2017 | 30 |
| 13 | 15/03/2017 | 40 |

So, first we need to highlight which days are the 1st and which are the 15th. We can do this, by adding the following DAY function to column C. In cell C2 type the following, then copy it down the rows.

=day(A2)

This has extracted just the days from the dates in column A.

| | A | B | C |
|---|---|---|---|
| 1 | | Num of students | Day |
| 2 | 01/10/2016 | 50 | 1 |
| 3 | 15/10/2016 | 80 | 15 |
| 4 | 01/11/2016 | 80 | 1 |
| 5 | 15/11/2016 | 90 | 15 |
| 6 | 01/12/2016 | 100 | 1 |
| 7 | 15/12/2016 | 50 | 15 |
| 8 | 01/01/2016 | 40 | 1 |
| 9 | 15/12/2016 | 80 | 15 |
| 10 | 01/02/2017 | 50 | 1 |
| 11 | 15/02/2017 | 80 | 15 |
| 12 | 01/03/2017 | 30 | 1 |
| 13 | 15/03/2017 | 40 | 15 |

Now we can add up those which are the 1st and those which are on the 15th.

| E | F | G |
|---|---|---|
| | 1st | 15th |
| Num of students | 350 | 420 |

To do this we use a SUMIF function (see chapter 7). Write the following in cell F1:

```
=sumif(C2:C13,"=1",B2:B13)
```

This looks in range C2:C13 and checks to see if there are any "1s", if there are it adds up the number of students in column B, that correspond. Similarly, we do the same for "15ths".

```
=sumif(C2:C13,"=15",B2:B13)
```

We can see above that the 15th has more students.

**Example 4 - Extracting the month or year / Find out how old someone is**

Similar to the DAY function, we can also use the MONTH and YEAR functions to extract the month and year from a date.

In cell A1, I have a birthday. In cell B1, I've added the MONTH function you can see in cell C1. This returns the month as a number from 1 to 12.

|   | A | B | C |
|---|---|---|---|
| 1 | 31/03/1973 | 3 | =MONTH(A1) |
| 2 |  | 1973 |  |
| 3 |  | 46 |  |
| 4 |  | 46 Years Old |  |

We can do the same with the year. In cell B2, I've added the YEAR function you can see in cell C2, and this returns the year.

|   | A | B | C |
|---|---|---|---|
| 1 | 31/03/1973 | 3 | =MONTH(A1) |
| 2 |  | 1973 | =YEAR(A1) |
| 3 |  | 46 |  |
| 4 |  | 46 Years Old |  |

Let's find out how old this person is. In cell B3, I've written the formula you can see in cell C3. This gets the year from today's date and then subtracts the year in cell A1, i.e. 2016-1973. It then returns the number of years.

|   | A | B | C |
|---|---|---|---|
| 1 | 31/03/1973 | 3 | =MONTH(A1) |
| 2 |  | 1973 | =YEAR(A1) |
| 3 |  | 46 | =YEAR(TODAY())-YEAR(A1) |
| 4 |  | 46 Years Old |  |

Similar to example 2, we can add some text to the number to make it more meaningful, by using the ampersand.

| | A | B | C |
|---|---|---|---|
| 1 | 31/03/1973 | 3 | =MONTH(A1) |
| 2 | | 1973 | =YEAR(A1) |
| 3 | | 46 | =YEAR(TODAY())-YEAR(A1) |
| 4 | | 46 Years Old | =YEAR(TODAY())-YEAR(A1)&" Years Old" |

The same applies for extracting times from a date and time. We have the HOUR, MINUTE and SECOND function which will extract the different parts of a time.

| | A | B | C |
|---|---|---|---|
| 1 | 13/11/2016 20:30 | 20 | =HOUR(A1) |
| 2 | | 30 | =MINUTE(A1) |
| 3 | | 0 | =SECOND(A1) |

As you can see, by themselves these functions are limited but when combined with other functions, they allow you to work with dates and calculate what you want.

# 15: WEEKDAY, WORKDAY, NETWORKDAYS, EDATE, EOMONTH, CHOOSE

Following on from the previous chapter on the basic date functions, let's look at some really useful functions that work with dates, namely: WEEKDAY, WORKDAY, NETWORKDAYS, EDATE and EOMONTH, plus we'll see an example with the CHOOSE function. With these we'll:

- Find out the day of the week of a particular date
- Work out a deadline date
- Work out how many working days there are between two dates
- Easily set up start and end of the month dates
- Work out how many days there are in a month
- Work out how many working days there are in a month

**Example 1 - What day of the week was a particular date?**

What day of the week was 1st January 2000 on? No, I couldn't remember either. Let's use the WEEKDAY function to quickly find out.

In cell A1 I've written the date, then in cell B1 I write the following:

=WEEKDAY(A1)

This returns the day number for that date, where Sunday=1 and Saturday=7. So, we can see that 1st January 2000 was in fact a Saturday.

| | A | B |
|---|---|---|
| 1 | 1/1/2000 | 7 |

Personally, I find using Sunday as the first day of the week a bit confusing, but you can change which day is the first one by adapting the formula. Let's make Monday the first day of the week. This time, after the date, add a comma then "2". This makes Monday the first day.

=WEEKDAY(A1,2)

As we can see in cell B2, it now returns "6", as Saturday is now the sixth day of the week.

| | A | B |
|---|---|---|
| 1 | 1/1/2000 | 7 |
| 2 | | 6 |

You can make any day the first day, just by changing the number in the formula.

**Example 2 - Returning the day of the week as text not as a number**

The above example's great, but it requires you to think of what the number represents. Wouldn't it be better to return the actual name of the day? Well, that's easily done by adding the CHOOSE function to our WEEKDAY one.

I write the following formula:

`=CHOOSE(WEEKDAY(A1,2),"Monday","Tuesday","Wednesday","Thursday","Friday","Saturday","Sunday")`

This carries out the WEEKDAY function, finds the day number, then looks down the list of days. So, for the 1st Jan 2000, it will move along 6 spaces down the list and then choose the entry there, which of course is Saturday. Note, each entry needs to be in quotation marks.

|   | A | B |
|---|---|---|
| 1 | 01/01/2000 | Saturday |

The entries can be anything you want. For example, the other day I used this to return the days in Spanish despite using a sheet that was English-based, as we have both English and Spanish speakers using it.

**Example 3 - Find out the date a number of days from a given date**

In this example, a team have 90 working days to finish the project. I want to find out want date that is. To do so, I use the WORKDAY function:

`=WORKDAY(B1,90)`

This takes the start date in cell B1 and then adds 90 working days, and returns the end date. So, I can quickly see that they need to finish by 22nd March.

|   | A | B |
|---|---|---|
| 1 | Today: | 16/11/2016 |
| 2 | Deadline (in 90 working days time): | 22/03/2017 |

What about the Christmas holidays I hear you cry?! Well, WORKDAY can exclude a list of dates, such as holidays. In range D2 to D4, I've listed the Christmas and New Year holidays.

|   | D | E |
|---|---|---|
|   | Holidays |   |
|   | 25/12/2016 | Sunday |
|   | 26/12/2016 | Monday |
|   | 01/01/2017 | Sunday |

Back in our formula, I need to state where those holidays are, so I just add them after the "90".

`=WORKDAY(B1,90,D2:D4)`

This time I see that the deadline's moved out a little. Note, it's only moved by one day, as out of 3 holidays, only one falls on a work day. In the UK, the weekend ones would in fact move to the Monday, but I just wanted to keep the example simple, and in other countries weekend public holidays don't always move.

|   | A | B |
|---|---|---|
| 1 | Today: | 16/11/2016 |
| 2 | Deadline (in 90 working days time): | 22/03/2017 |
| 3 | Deadline (inc working day holidays): | 23/03/2017 |

**Example 4 - How many working days are there between two dates?**

I'm looking forward to my Christmas break already and I want to know how more working days there are until I finish for Christmas. In cell B1 I put today's date, in cell B2 the end of term date.

|   | A | B |
|---|---|---|
| 1 | Today: | 17/11/2016 |
| 2 | End of term: | 22/12/2016 |
| 3 | Working days until end of term | 26 |

In cell B3, I write the following:

`=NETWORKDAYS(B1,B2)`

This takes the two dates and works out how many working days (Mon to Fri) there are. As we can see there are 26 days.

Ah, but in Spain we also have two public holidays on 6th and 8th December, I'm not working then.

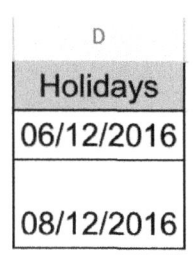

| D |
|---|
| Holidays |
| 06/12/2016 |
| 08/12/2016 |

We can exclude those from the total by modifying the formula:

`=NETWORKDAYS(B1,B2,D2:D4)`

This now works out the number of days and subtracts the number of days in range D2:D4. So, it turns out there are only 24 working days. Excellent!

| | A | B |
|---|---|---|
| 1 | Today: | 17/11/2016 |
| 2 | End of term: | 22/12/2016 |
| 3 | Working days until end of term | 26 |
| 4 | Working days until end of term (inc holidays) | 24 |

## Example 5 - Easily adding start of the month and end of the month dates

In the table below, I want to record how many students have had classes in each month. I need to include the start of the month and end of the month dates as I'm going to use them to filter a master list. Now, I could type in the dates, but with a long list this would be laborious. Instead I can use the EDATE and EOMONTH functions to do it for me.

| | A | B | C |
|---|---|---|---|
| 1 | Start of month | End of month | Number of students |
| 2 | 01/10/2016 | 31/10/2016 | 500 |
| 3 | 01/11/2016 | 30/11/2016 | 400 |
| 4 | 01/12/2016 | 31/12/2016 | 700 |
| 5 | 01/01/2017 | 31/01/2017 | 300 |
| 6 | 01/02/2017 | 28/02/2017 | 500 |

In cell A2 I write the first date I want, in this case 1/10/2016. then in cell B2, I want to add the end of that month. I do this by writing the following:

=EOMONTH(A2,0)

This takes the date in cell A2 and then gets the date of the end of the month and as it's the same month, I write a "0". If I wanted the next month (i.e. 30/11), I would write "1" and so on.

On the next line I want to add the start of the next month (1/11). So, I write the following:

=EDATE(A2,1)

This takes the date in cell A2 and adds a month to it, keeping the same day of the month, i.e. 1st. In cell B2, I copy the same EOMONTH function as before, i.e. from cell B2.

Now for all future rows I can just copy this row and paste it below. So, for example, cell A6 is =EDATE(A5,1) and cell B6 is =EOMONTH(B5,0).

You can use EOMONTH to return the end of the month of future months, just by changing the 0 to a higher number. For example, in cell B2 =EOMONTH(A2, 3) would return 31/1/2017.

**Example 6 - Working out the number of days in a month**

In a salary sheet, I need to know how many days there were in the month. Every month I type in the month in cell B1 and in cell B2 it tells me how many days are in that month, which I can then use in other formulas to calculate my teachers' salaries.

|   | A | B |
|---|---|---|
| 1 | Month: | 01/02/2016 |
| 2 | Days in the month: | 29 |

In cell B2, I write the following:

=eomonth(B1,0)-B1+1

This gets the date in cell B1 and gets the end of month date, then subtracts the start of the month (B1) then adds one so it starts with one and not zero.

As you can see it rightly, worked out that in 2016, February had 29 days.

**Example 7 - Working out the number of working days in a month**

In the same salary sheet, I also need to know how many working days there were in that month. This time I need to combine the NETWORKDAYS function with the EOMONTH function. I write the following in cell B3:

=NETWORKDAYS(B1,EOMONTH(B1,0))

This gets the start date from cell B1, gets the end of the month date from the EOMONTH function and works out the number of working days in between.

So, it correctly worked out that there were 21 working days in February 2016.

|   | A | B |
|---|---|---|
| 1 | Month: | 01/02/2016 |
| 2 | Days in the month: | 29 |
| 3 | Working days in the month: | 21 |

There are two additional functions similar to WORKDAY and NETWORKDAYS, these are WORKDAY.INTL and NETWORKDAYS.INTL. These add the extra option of stating how many days of the week are non-working.

# 16: GOOGLETRANSLATE, DETECTLANGUAGE

Lots of people know about and have used Google Translate either on their phones or on the Google website but what they often don't know is that there is a built-in function in Google Sheets, which will allow you to translate from one language to another, and even automatically recognise the language and translate it.

So, in this chapter we're going to look at the functions GOOGLETRANSLATE and DETECTLANGUAGE and you'll see how easy these are to use.

### Example 1 - Translating from one language to another

I created a system where I work, where teachers can report problems in their classrooms via Google Forms on their mobiles. We're in Seville, Spain, and some teachers can't speak Spanish very well, so I needed a system that would allow them to report the problems in English and then it would translate it into Spanish, so that the maintenance and IT guys, who don't speak English, can understand the problems and act on them.

To do this, I used the GOOGLETRANSLATE function. To show this, let's look at a simple example below. In cell A2 and I have the problem reported by the teacher in English, then the translation will appear in cell B2. In cell C2 I've written the formula that has been used.

|   | A | B | C |
|---|---|---|---|
| 1 | English | Spanish | Formula |
| 2 | The WIFI doesn't work. | El wifi no funciona. | =GOOGLETRANSLATE(A2, "en", "es") |

The GOOGLETRANSLATE function has 3 parts. First, the source text (here in cell A2), second, the source language (here English), and thirdly, the target language (here Spanish). Note, you have to use the codes "en" for English, "es" for Spanish (español). As you can see, it translated the original sentence fine.

### Example 2 - Detecting a language

The above example works fine for our English teachers, but in our department, we also have French, German, Portuguese, and Chinese teachers and not all of them speak good Spanish. So, how do allow them to use this in their own languages? This is where DETECTLANGUAGE comes in. This will look at the text and determine what language it is, then return the code for that language.

So, in cell A2 we have some text in English. in cell B2, we have the DETECTLANGUAGE function I've written in cell C2. As you can see, it's correctly returned that the text is in English.

|   | A | B | C |
|---|---|---|---|
| 1 | English | Spanish | Formula |
| 2 | The WIFI doesn't work. | en | =DETECTLANGUAGE(A2) |

### Example 3 - Detecting a language and translating it

Having the DETECTLANGUAGE function return the language is useful but really, we then need it to combine the GOOGLETRANSLATE one to automatically change from the various languages that the problems could be written in to Spanish.

So, in cell B2, we add the formula you can see in cell C2. Basically, we've replaced the source language part with the DETECTLANGUAGE function. So, it looks at the text in cell A2, then uses DETECTLANGUAGE to determine which language it is, then translates it to Spanish.

| | A | B | C |
|---|---|---|---|
| 1 | English | Spanish | Formula |
| 2 | The WIFI doesn't work. | El wifi no funciona. | =GOOGLETRANSLATE(A2,DETECTLANGUAGE(A2), "es") |

Here's the same but with the problem reported in French. As we'll see in the next example, Google Translate is good but at the moment it is still a long way off being perfect, as translating language is extremely complicated.

| | A | B | C |
|---|---|---|---|
| 1 | French | Spanish | Formula |
| 2 | Le WIFI ne fonctionne pas. | El WiFi no funciona. | =GOOGLETRANSLATE(A2,DETECTLANGUAGE(A2), "es") |

### Example 4 - Automatically translating board vocabulary

Another use of this is in the classroom, where in foreign language classes it's usual to record unknown vocabulary on the board during the lesson. I sometimes use a Google Doc and share it with the students, but here we can use a Google Sheet and it can translate the words automatically as I add them.

To do this, I have a Google Sheet with two columns. In column A I type the English words and phrases that come up. In column B, I have a GOOGLETRANSLATE formula copied down lots of rows, so that as I type in a word, the translation appears in the cell next to it.

| | A | B |
|---|---|---|
| 1 | English | Spanish |
| 2 | car | coche |
| 3 | nephew | sobrino |
| 4 | niece | sobrina |
| 5 | interesting | interesante |
| 6 | useful | útil |
| 7 | to drive | conducir |
| 8 | to have a coffee | para tomar un café |
| 9 | to go sightseeing | ir a ver paisajes |

I use the same formula as in example 1, except that I'm going from English to Spanish, but also, I wrap it up in an IFERROR function, just so that empty cells don't produce an error message, instead they just leave the cells in B blank.

```
=iferror(GOOGLETRANSLATE(A2, "en", "es"),"")
```

If you know some Spanish, you will notice that in fact some of the translations aren't that good, or at least will depend on the situation. So, as you can see it needs to be used with care, but this can also be used as a discussion point with your students.

**Example 5 - Having a conversation where neither person speaks the other's language**

This is a nice example where two people can have a conversation, despite not knowing each other's language. In this case, it was two children in different countries, using a Google Sheet to communicate with each other.

In the white cells they type their conversations, one line at a time going down the page. English on the left and the other in Spanish on the right. In the yellow part are the translations. The translations are good enough for them to communicate. They could of course use this to help them learn each other's language.

| | A | B | C | D |
|---|---|---|---|---|
| 1 | **English** | **Spanish Translation** | **English Translation** | **Spanish** |
| 2 | Hi Mercedes! | Hola Mercedes! | Barrie Hello! | Hola Barrie! |
| 3 | How are you? | ¿Cómo estás? | I'm fine. and you? | Estoy bien. ¿y tú? |
| 4 | I'm fine, thanks. What have you been doing today? | Estoy bien, gracias. ¿Que has estado haciendo hoy? | I went to the cinema to see the new James Bond film. | Fui al cine para ver la película nueva de James Bond. |
| 5 | Was it good? | ¿Era bueno? | Yes, but I prefer Sean Connery. | Sí, pero prefiero las de Sean Connery. |
| 6 | Me too. | Yo también. | What have you done today? | ¿Qué has hecho tú hoy? |
| 7 | I went to visit my grandparents. | Fui a visitar a mis abuelos. | Where they live? | ¿Dónde viven? |
| 8 | In south-east Wales. | En el sureste de Gales. | Are you away from home? | ¿Está lejos de tu casa? |
| 9 | A little. They live about 2 hours from my house. | Un poco. Ellos viven cerca de 2 horas de mi casa. | | |

In column B, I've written this formula down the rows:

```
=iferror(GOOGLETRANSLATE(A2,"en", "es"),"")
```

And in column C, I've written this one:

```
=iferror(GOOGLETRANSLATE(D2,"es", "en"),"")
```

Again, I've wrapped them up in the IFERROR function, so that it removes error messages.

In the GOOGLETRANSLATE we can also omit the source language and target language and let Sheets do it automatically. For example, in example 1 this function will look at cell A2, it will detect the language and then translate it to the language your Google account is in. This can be fine in many cases, but I prefer to be more prescriptive, just to avoid it coming up with strange results.

=GOOGLETRANSLATE(A2)

Also, we've only looked at single words and short sentences, but this works with long texts too.

Google Translate doesn't translate all of the 6,000+ languages in the world, but it does cover the most common ones. Here's a list of the language codes. This is continually being updated so new ones may not be on here.

| Language | Code | Language | Code | Language | Code | Language | Code |
|---|---|---|---|---|---|---|---|
| Afrikaans | af | Esperanto | eo | Irish | ga | Russian | ru |
| Albanian | sq | Estonian | et | Italian | it | Serbian | sr |
| Arabic | ar | Filipino | tl | Japanese | ja | Slovak | sk |
| Azerbaijani | az | Finnish | fi | Kannada | kn | Slovenian | sl |
| Basque | eu | French | fr | Korean | ko | Spanish | es |
| Bengali | bn | Galician | gl | Latin | la | Swahili | sw |
| Belarusian | be | Georgian | ka | Latvian | lv | Swedish | sv |
| Bulgarian | bg | German | de | Lithuanian | lt | Tamil | ta |
| Catalan | ca | Greek | el | Macedonian | mk | Telugu | te |
| Chinese Simplified | zh-CN | Gujarati | gu | Malay | ms | Thai | th |
| Chinese Traditional | zh-TW | Haitian Creole | ht | Maltese | mt | Turkish | tr |
| Croatian | hr | Hebrew | iw | Norwegian | no | Ukrainian | uk |
| Czech | cs | Hindi | hi | Persian | fa | Urdu | ur |
| Danish | da | Hungarian | hu | Polish | pl | Vietnamese | vi |
| Dutch | nl | Icelandic | is | Portuguese | pt | Welsh | cy |
| English | en | Indonesian | id | Romanian | ro | Yiddish | yi |

In summary, it's a great way to automatically translate within a document.

# 17: OFFSET

Sometimes we spend time setting up beautiful spreadsheets only for us to have to add rows or columns afterwards, which then messes up our formulas and we have to change them. In this chapter, we're going to look at a couple of examples of the OFFSET function, which will help us create more dynamic formulas. What we mean by this is that the formula will adapt to changes made to the spreadsheets, quite often where rows and columns have been added.

**Example 1 - Creating dynamic ranges to maintain an average formula**

Here we have some marks for some students. In cell B6 I've added an AVERAGE function to work out the average of the marks.

| | A | B |
|---|---|---|
| 1 | **Students** | **Marks** |
| 2 | Paul | 8 |
| 3 | John | 7 |
| 4 | George | 9 |
| 5 | Ringo | 10 |
| 6 | **Average** | **8.5** |

=AVERAGE(B2:B5)

But I now have another student to add who's done the test. I add a row and insert the student's details, but as you can see this hasn't changed the average figure.

| | A | B |
|---|---|---|
| 1 | **Students** | **Marks** |
| 2 | Paul | 8 |
| 3 | John | 7 |
| 4 | George | 9 |
| 5 | Ringo | 10 |
| 6 | Peter | 10 |
| 7 | **Average** | **8.5** |

If we look at the formula, it hasn't changed despite there being an extra row.

=AVERAGE(B2:B5)

We can solve this by using the OFFSET function in the AVERAGE one.

| D | E |
|---|---|
| **Students** | **Marks** |
| Paul | 8 |
| John | 7 |
| George | 9 |
| Ringo | 10 |
| **Average** | **8.5** |

In cell E6, I've added the following formula:

=AVERAGE(E2:OFFSET(E6,-1,0))

OK, so what's happening? Well let's look at the syntax of the function to understand it better.

```
=OFFSET(
```
OFFSET(cell_reference, offset_rows, offset_columns, [height], [width])

Example
OFFSET(A2, 3, 4, 2, 2)

Summary
Returns a range reference that shifts a specified number of rows and columns from a starting cell reference.

▸ cell_reference
The starting point from which to count the offset rows and columns.

offset_rows
The number of rows to offset by.

offset_columns
The number of columns to offset by.

height - [optional]
The height of the range to return starting at the offset target.

width - [optional]
The width of the range to return starting at the offset target.

Learn more about OFFSET

The OFFSET function has 3 main parts:

**cell reference**: this is the cell you start from

**offset rows**: this is the number of rows you move to; positive numbers move down and negative numbers move up. In other words, a positive number increases the row number and a negative one decreases it.

**offset columns**: this is the number of columns you move to

There are 2 other optional parts, height and width, but here we're not going to use them for now.

So, going back to our formula:

`=AVERAGE(E2:OFFSET(E6,-1,0))`

The OFFSET function starts at E6 which is where our total is.

Then moves up one row to E5 as there's a -1 in the second part.

It doesn't move from the column, as there's a 0 in the third part.

So, this returns the cell E5.

Now we just add the AVERAGE part. It takes the range from E2 to the result of the OFFSET function, which is E5 (E2:E5).

As we can see it returns the correct average like we saw earlier.

| Students | Marks |
|---|---|
| Paul | 8 |
| John | 7 |
| George | 9 |
| Ringo | 10 |
| **Average** | **8.5** |

Now let's add the extra student and see what happens. Ah-ha, the average has changed from 8.5 to 8.8, which is what we want.

| Students | Marks |
|---|---|
| Paul | 8 |
| John | 7 |
| George | 9 |
| Ringo | 10 |
| Peter | 10 |
| **Average** | **8.8** |

Looking at the formula, we can see that it has changed subtly, the start cell reference is now E7 (the total) and it's still moving one cell up, so returns the cell E6. This means the range is now E2:E6, which is what we want.

```
=AVERAGE(E2:OFFSET(E7,-1,0))
```

We can add or delete rows and the average will always be correct, without having to manually change it.

**Example 2 - Dynamically calculating the sales of the last X months**

Here we have a company's sales from January to June. The sales manager wants to be able to find out the sales for the last X months. Here he adds the number of months he wants to look back from the last month, e.g. in cell D1 he writes 2. Then in cell D2 it tells him the total number of sales in that period, which in this case is 1,400 (600+800).

|   | A | B | C | D |
|---|---|---|---|---|
| 1 | **Month** | **Sales** | Last X months: | 2 |
| 2 | Jan | 500 | Total sales in last X months: | 1400 |
| 3 | Feb | 400 | | |
| 4 | Mar | 800 | | |
| 5 | Apr | 700 | | |
| 6 | May | 600 | | |
| 7 | June | 800 | | |

So, how did we do that? In cell D2 is the following formula:

```
=SUM(OFFSET(B2,COUNT(B2:B)-D1,0,D1,1))
```

Let's break it down and start with the OFFSET function.

B2: This starts from cell B2 (the first month's sales).

COUNT(B2:B)-D1: Then it counts how many rows (months) there are from B2 to the end of column B. Then it takes away the number of months we want to report back, in this case 2. So it offsets by 4 rows (6-2), so starts from cell B6.

0: It doesn't move columns.

D1: The height is the figure in D1, i.e. 2 rows. So, it takes figures that are from B6 to B7 (i.e. 2 rows).

1: It returns just that one column.

So, when we change the number of months in cell D1, it returns the new number of sales. In this case, the last 3 months total 2,100.

|   | A | B | C | D |
|---|---|---|---|---|
| 1 | **Month** | **Sales** | Last X months: | 3 |
| 2 | Jan | 500 | Total sales in last X months: | 2100 |
| 3 | Feb | 400 | | |
| 4 | Mar | 800 | | |
| 5 | Apr | 700 | | |
| 6 | May | 600 | | |
| 7 | June | 800 | | |

This has the added benefit, like we saw in example 1, that when more rows are added it still works. Now, the sales manager has added the sales for the month of July. As we can see, the last 3 months now add up to 2,400.

|   | A | B | C | D |
|---|---|---|---|---|
| 1 | **Month** | **Sales** | Last X months: | 3 |
| 2 | Jan | 500 | Total sales in last X months: | 2400 |
| 3 | Feb | 400 | | |
| 4 | Mar | 800 | | |
| 5 | Apr | 700 | | |
| 6 | May | 600 | | |
| 7 | June | 800 | | |
| 8 | July | 1000 | | |

# 18: IMAGE

In this chapter let's look how we can insert images into our sheets. There are two main ways, either inserting the image via the Insert menu or by using the IMAGE function.

**Example 1 - Inserting an image from Drive**

Here let's add an image from my Drive. Open the "Insert" menu then click "Image". There are two options to choose from, 1) "Image in cell, or 2) Image over cells. Let's add it over the cells.

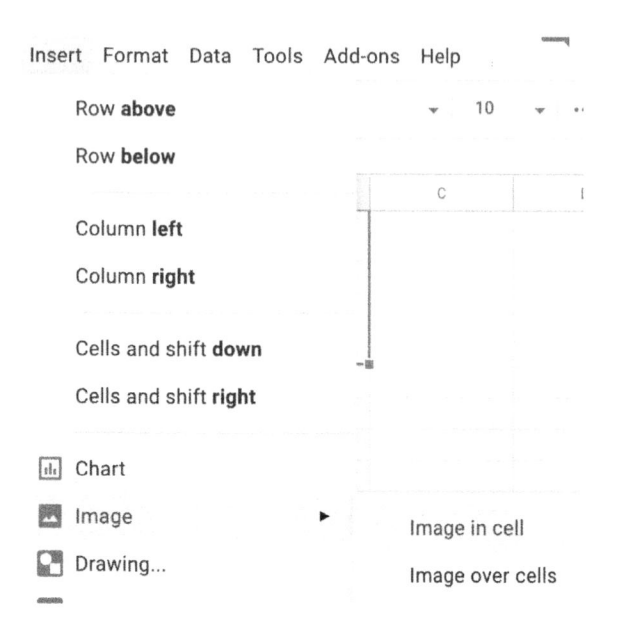

```
Insert  Format  Data  Tools  Add-ons  Help

        Row above                          10
        Row below
                                C        
        Column left
        Column right

        Cells and shift down
        Cells and shift right

   📊   Chart
   🖼   Image            ▶      Image in cell
   ✏   Drawing...              Image over cells
```

Choose where your image is, in this case, I'm uploading it from my computer.

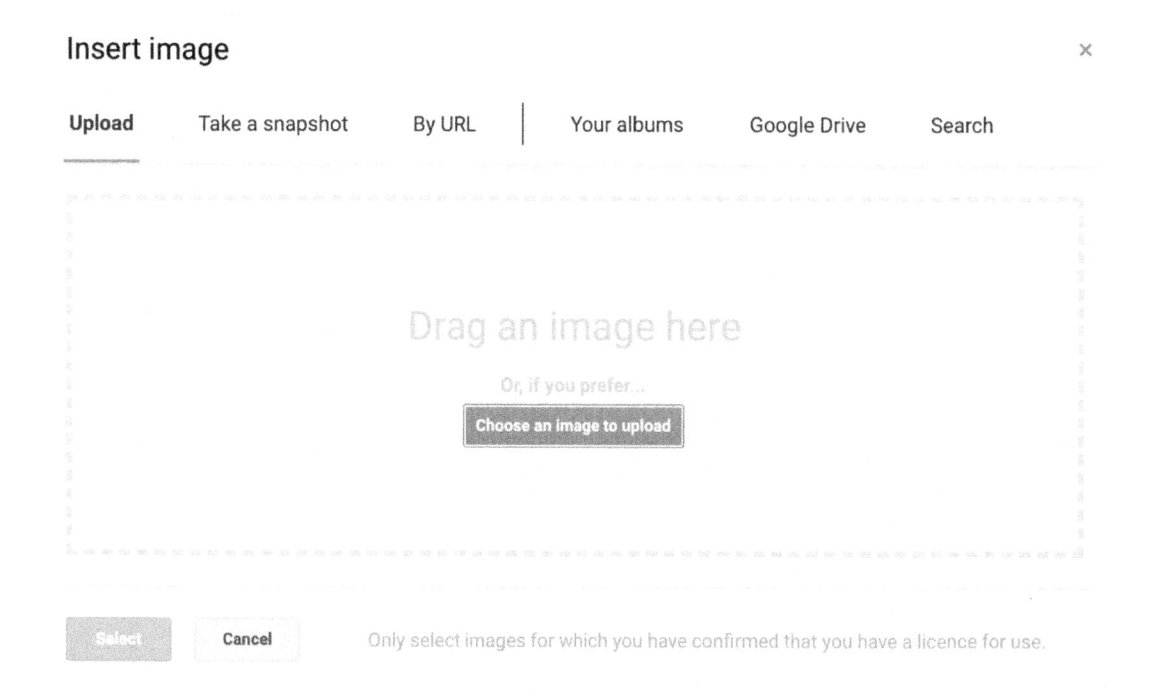

```
Insert image                                                    ×

Upload    Take a snapshot    By URL  |  Your albums    Google Drive    Search
──────


                        Drag an image here
                           Or, if you prefer...
                        [Choose an image to upload]




   [Select]    Cancel        Only select images for which you have confirmed that you have a licence for use.
```

Search for your image, and click on the one you want, then click Open.

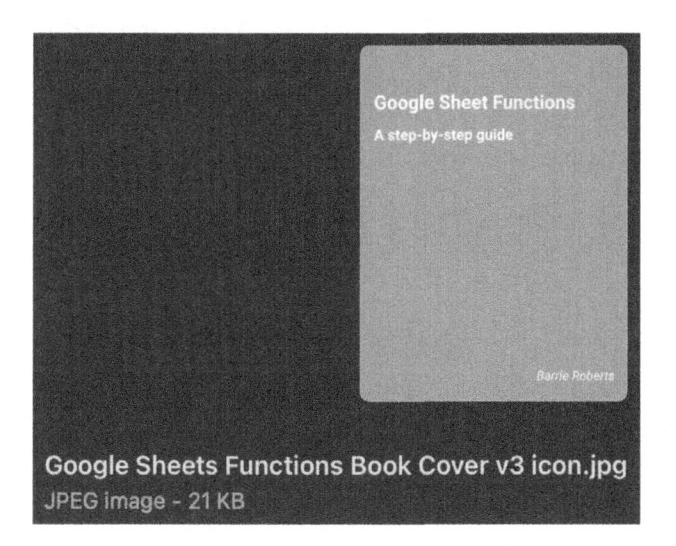

This will place the image on top of your sheet and won't affect the cells in any way. You can change the size of it by moving the blue squares on the border of your image.

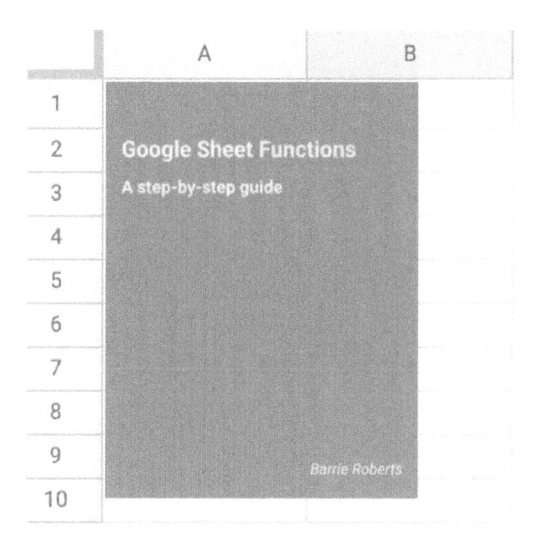

The other option is to add an image in cell, this adds the image within the cell. It's then affected by changes to the size of that cell.

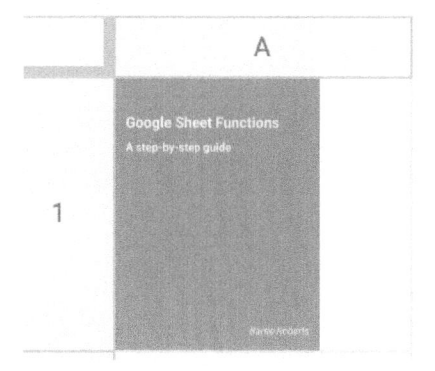

133                                                                                           18: IMAGE

**Example 2 - Inserting an image within a cell using the IMAGE function**

An alternative way to inserting images, is to use the IMAGE function, which will insert the image **within** the cell where that function is. To do this we need the URL of the image.

In the cell I type =IMAGE() then in between the brackets I add speech marks and the URL inside them, i.e. =IMAGE("www.google.com")

Here I'll add an image from my blog:

=IMAGE("https://www.bazroberts.com/wp-content/uploads/2021/09/Google-Sheets-Functions-Book-Cover-v3-icon.jpg")

This adds the image within the cell. A bit small, isn't it?

This is because it has adjusted the size of the image to the size of cell. To make it bigger we just make the row and/or column sizes bigger.

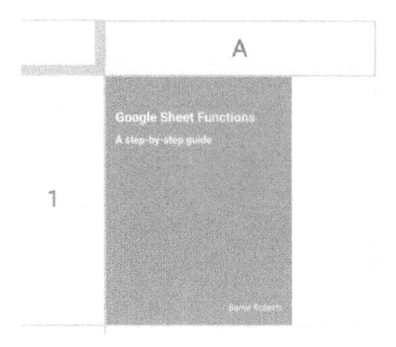

By default, the image is inserted in "sizing mode 1". So, what does that mean? Well, there are 4 modes and they treat the images in different ways.

Mode 1 - Resizes the image to fit inside the cell, **maintaining aspect ratio**.

Mode 2 - Stretches or compresses the image to fit inside the cell, **ignoring aspect ratio**.

Mode 3 - Leaves the image at **original size**, which **may cause cropping**.

Mode 4 - Allows the specification of a **custom size**.

So, let's look at the modes 2, 3, and 4 in turn.

Mode 2

Taking the same image and formula, but this time just adding a comma and 2 at the end, will squash the image into the cell, and ignore the original aspect ratio, so it now looks too wide.

=IMAGE("https://www.bazroberts.com/wp-content/uploads/2021/09/Google-Sheets-Functions-Book-Cover-v3-icon.jpg",2)

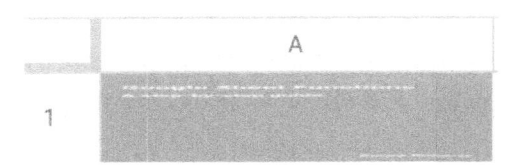

Mode 3

This time replacing the 2 with a 3, will insert the image as its original size, but if it is bigger than the cell, it will be cropped, as we can see below, it's chopped off the title text.

=IMAGE("https://www.bazroberts.com/wp-content/uploads/2021/09/Google-Sheets-Functions-Book-Cover-v3-icon.jpg",3)

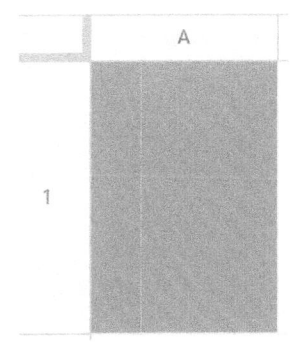

Mode 4

Finally, we can control the height and width we want, but to do this we must use mode 4. As you can see in the formula, after the 4, we add the height (150) and then the width (120).

=IMAGE("https://www.bazroberts.com/wp-content/uploads/2021/09/Google-Sheets-Functions-Book-Cover-v3-icon.jpg",4,150,120)

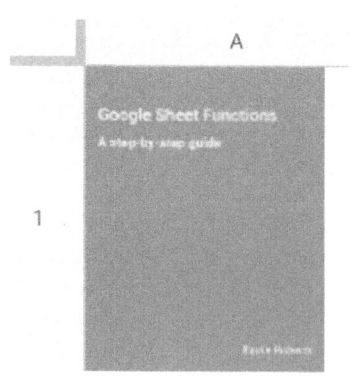

Which mode you use is of course entirely dependent on what you want to achieve. It's important to note that as these images are within the cells, they are affected by any cell changes, rows or columns added, etc.

# 19: ROUND, ROUNDUP, ROUNDDOWN

In this chapter, we're going to have a quick look at rounding numbers up and down, by using the ROUND, ROUNDUP, and ROUNDDOWN functions. The syntax is very easy, we tell the function the number we want to round and then to how many decimal places.

In cell A1 we have a number and in B2 we want to reduce it to just 2 decimal places. In cell B2 we write =ROUND(A1,2), this gets the number in cell A1 and then converts it to 2 decimal places.

|   | A | B | C |
|---|---|---|---|
| 1 | 3.5648 | 3.56 | =ROUND(A1,2) |

In the examples below we can see how the same formula treats numbers that are 0.5 or higher or less than 0.5. If the number is half or more it will round the number up, so 3.56 becomes 3.6, if we're working to 1 decimal place. If the number is less than half, it will round it down, so 3.14 becomes 3.1.

|   | A | B | C |
|---|---|---|---|
| 3 | 3.56 | 3.6 | =ROUND(A3,1) |
| 4 | 3.14 | 3.1 | =ROUND(A4,1) |

We can control whether we want it to round up or down. To always round it up, we use the ROUNDUP function in the same way as before. As you can see, it's rounded both figures up this time.

|   | A | B | C |
|---|---|---|---|
| 6 | 3.56 | 3.6 | =ROUNDUP(A6,1) |
| 7 | 3.14 | 3.2 | =ROUNDUP(A7,1) |

To always round down, we use the ROUNDDOWN function in the same way:

|   | A | B | C |
|---|---|---|---|
| 9 | 3.56 | 3.5 | =ROUNDDOWN(A9,1) |
| 10 | 3.14 | 3.1 | =ROUNDDOWN(A10,1) |

If you want to round whole numbers up, for example, to the nearest thousand, use a negative number. Here I'm rounding to the nearest thousand, by adding a -3.

|   | A | B | C |
|---|---|---|---|
| 12 | 234,545 | 235,000 | =ROUND(A12,-3) |

# 20: HYPERLINK

Here let's take a quick look at the HYPERLINK function, which allows you to add hyperlinks with ease and to also rename them.

Here I've just copied and pasted my blog address into the cell.

|   | A | B |
|---|---|---|
| 1 | https://www.bazroberts.com/ |   |

This is fine, but sometimes we don't want an ugly URL in our sheet. For example, I can change what shows by using the HYPERLINK function.

**Example 1 – Renaming a hyperlink**

Using the HYPERLINK function, I add the URL between speech marks, then after the comma, add the text I want visible on the sheet, again in speech marks.

```
=HYPERLINK("https://www.bazroberts.com/","MY BLOG")
```

Now in cell A1, I have the text I want.

|   | A |
|---|---|
| 1 | MY BLOG |

When you hover over the text, you can see that it's linked to a URL and clicking on the blue link, will take you to the webpage. It also gives you some extra information about the link.

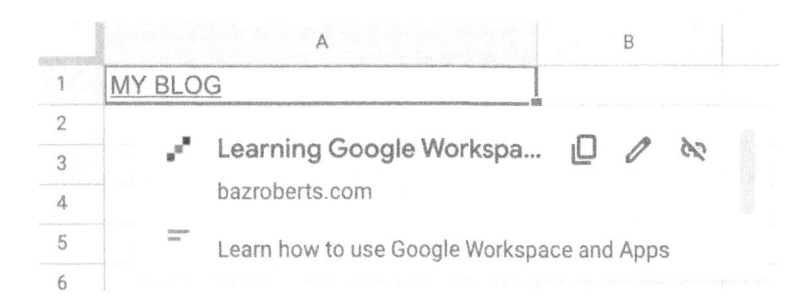

|   | A | B |
|---|---|---|
| 1 | MY BLOG |   |
| 2 |   |   |
| 3 | Learning Google Workspa... |   |
| 4 | bazroberts.com |   |
| 5 | Learn how to use Google Workspace and Apps |   |
| 6 |   |   |

## Example 2 – Linking to a Google Document

You can easily add links to documents on your Drive, just by adding the document URL in the HYPERLINK function.

```
=HYPERLINK("https://docs.google.com/document/d/1FILmMGheVWeSvFedG9nocy-pZYq1ZXstbNr1jdGlSDQ/edit","LINK")
```

Just make sure the person using your sheet, has access to the document.

## Example 3 – Linking to a particular sheet

We can also link to other sheets within the spreadsheet. To do this, open the sheet you want to link to and then copy the sheet ID which is at the end of the URL, after /edit. It will start with #gid=.

`28/edit#gid=1047778997`

Add that to the HYPERLINK function.

```
=HYPERLINK("#gid=1047778997","Link to Sheet 2")
```

This will now provide you with a link to that sheet. It's a useful way to navigate around your spreadsheet, especially if you have a lot of sheets.

**Example 4 – Linking to a particular cell**

Not only can we link to a sheet but we can also link to a particular cell.

Here I want to link to a list of books on Sheet 2 and starts in cell A3.

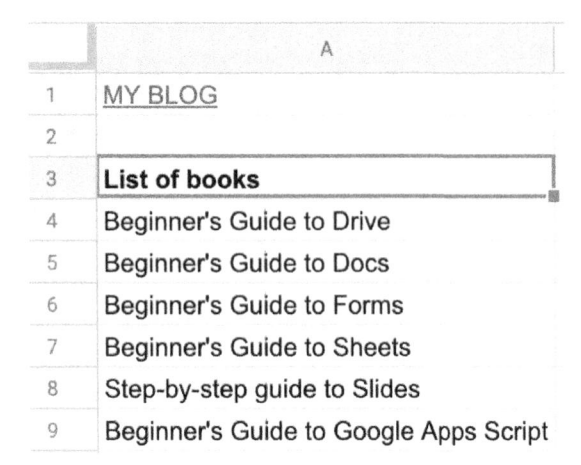

|   | A |
|---|---|
| 1 | MY BLOG |
| 2 |   |
| 3 | **List of books** |
| 4 | Beginner's Guide to Drive |
| 5 | Beginner's Guide to Docs |
| 6 | Beginner's Guide to Forms |
| 7 | Beginner's Guide to Sheets |
| 8 | Step-by-step guide to Slides |
| 9 | Beginner's Guide to Google Apps Script |

Right click on the cell and select "Get link to this cell".

> Insert link
>
> Get link to this cell

This will copy the link to the clipboard.

> Link copied to the clipboard.     ✕

On the sheet you want to add the link on, start typing the HYPERLINK function up until the first speech mark.

`=HYPERLINK("`

Then press Ctrl+V to paste the link. Then complete the HYPERLINK function in the normal way.

`=HYPERLINK("https://docs.google.com/spreadsheets/d/1yYQa95JPNlI4cQF1jM9bcuQ_BNKeoGeQoQa1oahfb28/edit#gid=1047778997&range=A3","List of books")`

You will notice that at the end of the URL, you have a reference to the sheet ID and then the cell range, in this case, A3.

`/edit#gid=1047778997&range=A3`

140                                                20: HYPERLINK

Add the wording in the link you want to see:

`7&range=A3","List of books")`

You see the link in the cell.

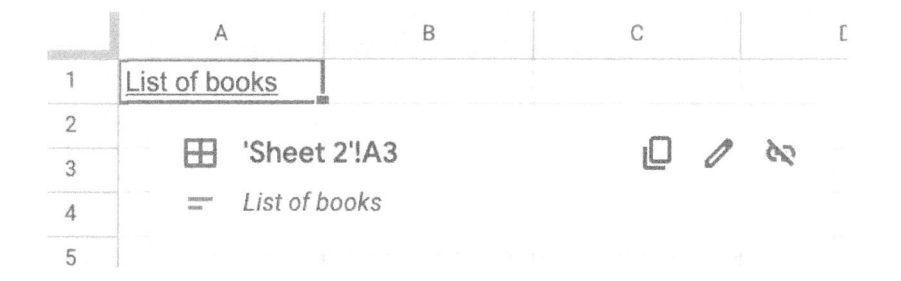

|   | A | B | C | D |
|---|---|---|---|---|
| 1 | List of books | | | |
| 2 | | | | |
| 3 | ▦ 'Sheet 2'!A3 | | | |
| 4 | = List of books | | | |
| 5 | | | | |

Clicking on the link will take you to Sheet 2 and cell A3.

|   | A |
|---|---|
| 1 | MY BLOG |
| 2 | |
| 3 | **List of books** |
| 4 | Beginner's Guide to Drive |
| 5 | Beginner's Guide to Docs |
| 6 | Beginner's Guide to Forms |
| 7 | Beginner's Guide to Sheets |
| 8 | Step-by-step guide to Slides |
| 9 | Beginner's Guide to Google Apps Script |

# 21: INDEX and MATCH

In chapter 5, we looked at how we can quickly look up tables for certain information, using the VLOOKUP function. This function is great but it does have some limitations. Firstly, when you look up information in the table you always have to look to the **right** for the matching information. Secondly, if you add a new column to the table, this messes up the references and it returns the wrong information.

This is where the functions INDEX and MATCH come in. With a combination of these two, you can look either left or right in a table, and it adapts to any added columns.

**INDEX**

First, let's see how the INDEX function works. Here we have 2 columns of data (columns A and B), we can pick out a certain cell's data by referring to its position in the table of data.

|   | A | B | C |
|---|---|---|---|
| 1 | 10 | 100 | 300 |
| 2 | 20 | 200 |   |
| 3 | 30 | 300 |   |

First we state the table range (A1:B3), then state the row number we want (3), then the column number (2). This returns the value in the cell (300).

=INDEX(A1:B3,3,2)

**INDEX and MATCH**
**Example 1 - Finding the classroom a specific teacher is in**

Usually, we don't already know the exact row and column we want, and this is where MATCH comes in.

Here we have a table which continues a list of teachers and which classroom they are in. I want to be able to type in cell D1 and find the classroom the teacher is in, and return it in cell D2.

|   | A | B | C | D |
|---|---|---|---|---|
| 1 | **Teacher** | **Classroom** | **Teacher:** | Barney |
| 2 | Fred | A1 | **Classroom:** | A3 |
| 3 | Wilma | A2 | | |
| 4 | Barney | A3 | | |
| 5 | Betty | A4 | | |
| 6 | John | B1 | | |
| 7 | Bob | B2 | | |
| 8 | Brian | B3 | | |
| 9 | Roseanne | B4 | | |

First, we need to understand the following MATCH function.

`=MATCH(D1,A2:A9,0)`

This looks for the teacher's name in D1 within the list of names (A2:A9). The 0 at the end looks for an exact match. This returns the number 3, as that is the number of places down the list in which Barney is. Now we have the row, we need to use that to find the classroom.

We do this by adding the INDEX function. This looks down the classroom list (range B2:B9), and picks the value at the place returned by the MATCH function. This is 3 as we saw above. This is classroom A3.

`=INDEX(B2:B9,MATCH(D1,A2:A9,0))`

So, to reiterate that, the first range (B2:B9) is the column you want to return the value from. The second range (A2:A9) is the column you want to initially search in.

In this example, we could have used the following VLOOKUP function, which as you can see returns the same result in cell E2.

`=VLOOKUP(D1,A2:B9,2,FALSE)`

**Example 2 - Finding who is in a particular classroom (looking up to the LEFT in a table)**

In the above example, we looked up a teacher and then moved RIGHT, to look up the classroom. But what happens if we want to do the opposite and look up the classroom and move LEFT and find out which teacher is in that room?

|   | A | B | C | D | E |
|---|---|---|---|---|---|
| 1 | Teacher | Classroom | Classroom: | A4 | |
| 2 | Fred | A1 | Teacher: | Betty | #N/A |
| 3 | Wilma | A2 | | | |
| 4 | Barney | A3 | | | |
| 5 | Betty | A4 | | | |
| 6 | John | B1 | | | |
| 7 | Bob | B2 | | | |
| 8 | Brian | B3 | | | |
| 9 | Roseanne | B4 | | | |

In cell E2, we have the following VLOOKUP formula and as we can see above, it returns a N/A error. This is because VLOOKUP cannot look left, as the column number is always positive, i.e. moves to the right.

`=vlookup(D1,A2:B9,1,FALSE)`

To be able to do it, in cell D2 we can use the following INDEX and MATCH formula:

`=INDEX(A2:A9,MATCH(D1,B2:B9,0))`

Here all we do is swap the formula we saw earlier around. We return the teacher in range A2:A9 by matching the classroom in range B2:B9.

**Example 3 - The effect of inserting a column in a table on an INDEX/MATCH and a VLOOKUP formula**

Another problem with using the VLOOKUP formula is that if a column is added and deleted from the table being used, it returns the wrong result, as the column reference is then incorrect.

Below we have started with the same table and formulas that we had in example 1. Then I have added a new column with the class year in those classrooms. As we can see, the INDEX/MATCH formula in cell E2, correctly returns that the Bob is in classroom B2. The VLOOKUP formula in cell F2, returns the class year and not the classroom.

|   | A | B | C | D | E | F |
|---|---|---|---|---|---|---|
| 1 | Teacher | Year | Classroom | Teacher: | Bob | |
| 2 | Fred | 1 | A1 | Classroom: | B2 | 6 |
| 3 | Wilma | 2 | A2 | | | |
| 4 | Barney | 3 | A3 | | | |
| 5 | Betty | 4 | A4 | | | |
| 6 | John | 5 | B1 | | | |
| 7 | Bob | 6 | B2 | | | |
| 8 | Brian | 7 | B3 | | | |
| 9 | Roseanne | 8 | B4 | | | |

As we can see, the VLOOKUP formula, still refers to the second column even though the range now covers 3 columns and we in fact now want the third column.

=vlookup(E1,A2:C9,2,FALSE)

Whereas, the INDEX/MATCH formula, adapts and looks up the classroom now in column C.

=INDEX(C2:C9,MATCH(E1,A2:A9,0))

**Example 4 - Returning more than one column of information**

We're not limited to just returning a cell in one specific column, we can return multiple columns or an entire row if we want. Here I want to return both the class year (in E2) and classroom (in F2), when the teacher is entered in cell D2.

|   | A | B | C | D | E | F |
|---|---|---|---|---|---|---|
| 1 | Teacher | Year | Classroom | Teacher | Year | Classroom |
| 2 | Fred | 1 | A1 | Bob | 6 | B2 |
| 3 | Wilma | 2 | A2 |   |   |   |
| 4 | Barney | 3 | A3 |   |   |   |
| 5 | Betty | 4 | A4 |   |   |   |
| 6 | John | 5 | B1 |   |   |   |
| 7 | Bob | 6 | B2 |   |   |   |
| 8 | Brian | 7 | B3 |   |   |   |
| 9 | Roseanne | 8 | B4 |   |   |   |

We use the following formula:

=INDEX(B2:C9,MATCH(D2,A2:A9,0))

Here the output range is B2:C9, which includes both the year and classroom. Note, that this returns the information, in separate columns to the right of the cell with the formula in it, i.e. cells E2 and F2.

**Example 5 - Matching a range and not an exact figure**

So far, we've been looking for exact matches, but like VLOOKUP we can also match within ranges.

Here we have a level test where the score corresponds with the student's level. If they get between 12 and 15 they are intermediate, and so on. In cell D1, we'll add the score, then in D2 we'll see the level.

|   | A | B | C | D |
|---|---|---|---|---|
| 1 | **Level** | **Min. Score** | **Score:** | 14 |
| 2 | Beginner | 5 | **Level:** | Intermediate |
| 3 | Elementary | 8 | | |
| 4 | Pre-Int | 10 | | |
| 5 | Intermediate | 12 | | |
| 6 | Upper-Int | 15 | | |
| 7 | Pre-Advanced | 16 | | |
| 8 | Advanced | 20 | | |
| 9 | Proficiency | 25 | | |

We use the following formula:

=INDEX(A2:A9,MATCH(D1,B2:B9,1))

This is the same as we've seen before, except that there is a "1" at the end this time. This time it's looking for 14 in column B and looks for the largest value that is the same or less than it. As 14 doesn't appear, it finds that 12 is the largest value. Then it returns the corresponding level in column A. So, basically, you can imagine a range from 12-14 for Intermediate, and that our value falls within that range.

There are 3 number options at the end of the formula:

1: causes MATCH to assume that the range is sorted in **ascending order** and return the **largest value less than** or **equal** to search_key.

0: indicates **exact** match, and is required in situations where range is not sorted.

-1: causes MATCH to assume that the range is sorted in **descending order** and return the **smallest value greater than** or **equal** to search_key.

So, if the list was sorted in descending order, we would use a "-1" instead. By default, "1" is used, so it is possible to leave the number out if you want to search a list in ascending order, like we did in this example.

In many cases VLOOKUP will do the job, but as you can see above there are times when INDEX and MATCH is better. It's less used partly because it looks more complicated but as we've seen above it's easy to set up.

# 22: QUERY

The QUERY function is in a category all on its own. It's an extremely powerful function that will let you filter, sort, group, pivot, basically extract data from a table and present it in numerous ways. At first it can look daunting, with its own language and syntax, but once you step your toe into the QUERY pool you'll realise that things are not so complicated and that with just one function, you can extract and analyse your data with ease.

As always, the best way to learn how to use it is through examples, and in this chapter, we're going to use two main sources of data, some questionnaire feedback, and some data from a HR department, building the complexity up step by step.

**Analysing questionnaire feedback**

Here we've used a Google Form to collect feedback on the teachers, the classrooms, and admin information at the end of every course in an academy. Each row is a student's piece of feedback. They grade the various criteria from 1 to 5, 5 being 'excellent'. Below is a snapshot of that table of data.

| | A | B | C | D | E | F | G | H | I | J | K | L | M | N |
|---|---|---|---|---|---|---|---|---|---|---|---|---|---|---|
| 1 | timestamp | Level | Teacher's name | Is clear | Is organized | Caters to my needs | Corrects my mistakes | Is punctual | Classroom | Comfort | Equipment | Course information | Payment information | The service in the office was ... |
| 2 | 04/07/2016 20:44:23 | A2 | Fred | 5 | 5 | 5 | 5 | 5 | A1 | 2 | 4 | 4 | 5 | 5 |
| 3 | 05/07/2016 19:19:38 | B2 | Betty | 5 | 5 | 5 | 4 | 5 | A5 | 3 | 2 | 3 | 5 | 5 |
| 4 | 06/07/2016 10:58:44 | B1 | Wilma | 5 | 5 | 5 | 5 | 5 | A3 | 5 | 5 | 4 | 5 | 5 |
| 5 | 06/07/2016 13:20:59 | A1 | Barney | 5 | 5 | 5 | 5 | 5 | A2 | 4 | 4 | 4 | 4 | 4 |
| 6 | 07/07/2016 12:08:08 | A2 | Wilma | 5 | 5 | 5 | 5 | 5 | A2 | 4 | 5 | 5 | 5 | 5 |
| 7 | 08/07/2016 16:08:36 | B1 | Betty | 5 | 5 | 5 | 5 | 5 | A5 | 4 | 3 | 2 | 4 | 5 |
| 8 | 13/07/2016 20:03:35 | B1 | Fred | 4 | 4 | 5 | 4 | 4 | A4 | 4 | 3 | 2 | 4 | 4 |

In the next few examples, we'll see how easy it is to analyse this data, each time with just one QUERY function.

**Example 1 - Selecting the relevant data from the master data**

The head of studies wants to look at the feedback for her teachers, and she doesn't need to know the classroom feedback or the admin feedback. So, the info she needs is from column A to H, as shown below:

| | A | B | C | D | E | F | G | H |
|---|---|---|---|---|---|---|---|---|
| 1 | timestamp | Level | Teacher's name | Is clear | Is organized | Caters to my needs | Corrects my mistakes | Is punctual |
| 2 | 04/07/2016 20:44:23 | A2 | Fred | 5 | 5 | 5 | 5 | 5 |
| 3 | 05/07/2016 19:19:38 | B2 | Betty | 5 | 5 | 5 | 4 | 5 |
| 4 | 06/07/2016 10:58:44 | B1 | Wilma | 5 | 5 | 5 | 5 | 5 |
| 5 | 06/07/2016 13:20:59 | A1 | Barney | 5 | 5 | 5 | 5 | 5 |
| 6 | 07/07/2016 12:08:08 | A2 | Wilma | 5 | 5 | 5 | 5 | 5 |
| 7 | 08/07/2016 16:08:36 | B1 | Betty | 5 | 5 | 5 | 5 | 5 |
| 8 | 13/07/2016 20:03:35 | B1 | Fred | 4 | 4 | 5 | 4 | 4 |
| 9 | 27/08/2016 09:13:05 | C1 | Barney | 5 | 4 | 5 | 5 | 5 |

In cell A1 on a different page, I've written the following QUERY function:

```
=query(Questionnaire!A1:N,"select A, B, C, D, E, F, G, H")
```

There are 2 main parts to a QUERY function, 1) the data range (in orange), 2) the query (in green)

So, in the first part we look at the page called "Questionnaire" and range A1 to column N (note this is an open-ended range as we will receive more entries in the future).

In the second part, we tell the function what to select. So, in this example, we want columns A to H. We add the column letters followed by commas. The query part always needs to be within speech marks, so we put it before select and at the end before the bracket.

"select" is one of the keywords within the QUERY language which tells the function what to do. Here are some of the other ones, most of which we will see in the following examples.

| Clause | Usage |
| --- | --- |
| select | Selects which columns to return, and in what order. If omitted, all of the table's columns are returned, in their default order. |
| where | Returns only rows that match a condition. If omitted, all rows are returned. |
| group by | Aggregates values across rows. |
| pivot | Transforms distinct values in columns into new columns. |
| order by | Sorts rows by values in columns. |
| limit | Limits the number of returned rows. |
| offset | Skips a given number of first rows. |
| label | Sets column labels. |
| format | Formats the values in certain columns using given formatting patterns. |
| options | Sets additional options. |

### Example 2a - Filter by a teacher's name

Now the head has decided that he wants to look at the feedback of a particular teacher. She wants the following information:

|   | A | B | C | D | E | F | G | H |
|---|---|---|---|---|---|---|---|---|
| 1 |   | Teacher: | Fred |   |   |   |   |   |
| 2 | timestamp | Level | Teacher's name | Is clear | Is organized | Caters to my needs | Corrects my mistakes | Is punctual |
| 3 | 04/07/2016 20:44:23 | A2 | Fred | 5 | 5 | 5 | 5 | 5 |
| 4 | 13/07/2016 20:03:35 | B1 | Fred | 4 | 4 | 5 | 4 | 4 |
| 5 | 28/08/2016 09:37:03 | B1 | Fred | 5 | 5 | 5 | 5 | 5 |
| 6 | 28/08/2016 09:40:35 | A2 | Fred | 5 | 5 | 5 | 5 | 5 |
| 7 | 29/08/2016 10:53:31 | B1 | Fred | 5 | 4 | 5 | 5 | 5 |
| 8 | 29/08/2016 11:25:06 | B2 | Fred | 5 | 5 | 5 | 5 | 5 |
| 9 | 27/09/2016 10:07:01 | C1 | Fred | 5 | 5 | 5 | 4 | 5 |
| 10 | 28/09/2016 10:26:21 | B1 | Fred | 4 | 3 | 4 | 3 | 3 |
| 11 | 28/09/2016 11:55:57 | A1 | Fred | 4 | 3 | 3 | 3 | 3 |
| 12 | 28/09/2016 13:44:29 | B2 | Fred | 4 | 4 | 4 | 4 | 4 |
| 13 | 30/11/2016 09:39:54 | C1 | Fred | 4 | 4 | 4 | 4 | 4 |
| 14 | 30/11/2016 09:46:11 | C2 | Fred | 4 | 3 | 4 | 3 | 3 |

Here's the QUERY formula I entered in cell A2:

`=query(Questionnaire!A1:N,"select A, B, C, D, E, F, G, H where C='Fred'")`

It's the same as before except that at the end I've stated a condition:

`where C='Fred'`

This looks at column C and returns anything that matches "Fred". I.e. it only returns the feedback for Fred.

### Example 2b - Filter by a teacher's name using a cell reference

The head has decided that she doesn't want to have to change the teacher's name within the formula every time she wants to look at the feedback of a different teacher, she wants to enter the teacher's name in cell B1 and wants the formula to update accordingly.

That's no problem, although the syntax looks a little ugly. Here's the formula:

`=query(Questionnaire!A1:N,"select A, B, C, D, E, F, G, H where C='"&B1&"'")`

At the end, instead of the name "Fred" I've put the reference to the cell. In QUERY function, you have to use this syntax: '"&B1&"' so it knows it's a cell reference.

`where C='"&B1&"'`

As you can see it produces the same information as before and now if the head wants to see another teacher's feedback, she only needs to change the name in cell B1.

|   | A | B | C | D | E | F | G | H |
|---|---|---|---|---|---|---|---|---|
| 1 |  | Teacher: | Fred |  |  |  |  |  |
| 2 | timestamp |  | Level | Teacher's name | Is clear | Is organized | Caters to my needs | Corrects my mistakes | Is punctual |
| 3 | 04/07/2016 20:44:23 | A2 | Fred | 5 | 5 | 5 | 5 | 5 |
| 4 | 13/07/2016 20:03:35 | B1 | Fred | 4 | 4 | 5 | 4 | 4 |
| 5 | 28/08/2016 09:37:03 | B1 | Fred | 5 | 5 | 5 | 5 | 5 |
| 6 | 28/08/2016 09:40:35 | A2 | Fred | 5 | 5 | 5 | 5 | 5 |
| 7 | 29/08/2016 10:53:31 | B1 | Fred | 5 | 4 | 5 | 5 | 5 |
| 8 | 29/08/2016 11:25:06 | B2 | Fred | 5 | 5 | 5 | 5 | 5 |
| 9 | 27/09/2016 10:07:01 | C1 | Fred | 5 | 5 | 5 | 4 | 5 |
| 10 | 28/09/2016 10:26:21 | B1 | Fred | 4 | 3 | 4 | 3 | 3 |
| 11 | 28/09/2016 11:55:57 | A1 | Fred | 4 | 3 | 3 | 3 | 3 |
| 12 | 28/09/2016 13:44:29 | B2 | Fred | 4 | 4 | 4 | 4 | 4 |
| 13 | 30/11/2016 09:39:54 | C1 | Fred | 4 | 4 | 4 | 4 | 4 |
| 14 | 30/11/2016 09:46:11 | C2 | Fred | 4 | 3 | 4 | 3 | 3 |

**Example 2c - Filter by a teacher's name and sort the date in descending order**

By default, the data is sorted from the oldest date to the most recent, but when there is a lot of data this means that to see the most recent and probably most relevant data, the person has to scroll down. We can remedy that easily by sorted the data by date in descending order, as we can see below:

|   | A | B | C | D | E | F | G |
|---|---|---|---|---|---|---|---|
| 1 |  | Teacher: | Fred |  |  |  |  |
| 2 | timestamp |  | Level | Is clear | Is organized | Caters to my needs | Corrects my mistakes | Is punctual |
| 3 | 30/11/2016 09:46:11 | C2 | 4 | 3 | 4 | 3 | 3 |
| 4 | 30/11/2016 09:39:54 | C1 | 4 | 4 | 4 | 4 | 4 |
| 5 | 28/09/2016 13:44:29 | B2 | 4 | 4 | 4 | 4 | 4 |
| 6 | 28/09/2016 11:55:57 | A1 | 4 | 3 | 3 | 3 | 3 |
| 7 | 28/09/2016 10:26:21 | B1 | 4 | 3 | 4 | 3 | 3 |
| 8 | 27/09/2016 10:07:01 | C1 | 5 | 5 | 5 | 4 | 5 |
| 9 | 29/08/2016 11:25:06 | B2 | 5 | 5 | 5 | 5 | 5 |
| 10 | 29/08/2016 10:53:31 | B1 | 5 | 4 | 5 | 5 | 5 |
| 11 | 28/08/2016 09:40:35 | A2 | 5 | 5 | 5 | 5 | 5 |
| 12 | 28/08/2016 09:37:03 | B1 | 5 | 5 | 5 | 5 | 5 |
| 13 | 13/07/2016 20:03:35 | B1 | 4 | 4 | 5 | 4 | 4 |
| 14 | 04/07/2016 20:44:23 | A2 | 5 | 5 | 5 | 5 | 5 |

To achieve this, I've used the same formula as before except at the end I've added an ORDER BY part:

=query(Questionnaire!A1:N,"select A, B, D, E, F, G, H where C='"&B1&"' order by A desc")

```
order by A desc
```

This orders (or sorts) column A (the dates) and the '*desc*' tells it to do it in descending order. If you want to tell it to do it in ascending order, write *asc*.

Carefully note the syntax, as one tiny error will stop this from working.

Also note that, the QUERY results aren't formatted and the column widths aren't automatically adjusted. This needs to be done manually either beforehand, or afterwards.

**Example 3a - Filter the data between 2 dates**

The head also wants to be able to filter the data for a particular period of time, e.g. September 16. As you can see below, the data has been filtered between 1/9/2016 and 30/9/2016.

|    | A | B | C | D | E | F | G | H |
|----|---|---|---|---|---|---|---|---|
| 1  |   | Teacher: | Fred | Start date: | 01/09/2016 | Finish date: | 30/09/2016 | |
| 2  | timestamp | Level | Teacher's name | Is clear | Is organized | Caters to my needs | Corrects my mistakes | Is punctual |
| 3  | 27/09/2016 09:59:11 | B2 | Betty | 5 | 5 | 5 | 5 | 5 |
| 4  | 27/09/2016 10:07:01 | C1 | Fred | 5 | 5 | 5 | 4 | 5 |
| 5  | 27/09/2016 10:11:39 | B2 | Barney | 5 | 5 | 5 | 5 | 5 |
| 6  | 28/09/2016 10:17:13 | B1 | Wilma | 4 | 3 | 3 | 3 | 2 |
| 7  | 28/09/2016 10:26:21 | B1 | Fred | 4 | 3 | 4 | 3 | 3 |
| 8  | 28/09/2016 11:48:14 | A2 | Barney | 3 | 3 | 4 | 1 | 1 |
| 9  | 28/09/2016 11:55:57 | A1 | Fred | 4 | 3 | 3 | 3 | 3 |
| 10 | 28/09/2016 12:09:47 | A2 | Barney | 5 | 5 | 5 | 5 | 5 |
| 11 | 28/09/2016 12:19:02 | A2 | Betty | 5 | 5 | 5 | 5 | 5 |
| 12 | 28/09/2016 13:43:19 | B1 | Barney | 5 | 5 | 5 | 5 | 4 |
| 13 | 28/09/2016 13:44:29 | B2 | Fred | 4 | 4 | 4 | 4 | 4 |
| 14 | 28/09/2016 13:44:54 | B1 | Wilma | 5 | 5 | 5 | 5 | 5 |
| 15 | 28/09/2016 15:41:47 | B1 | Barney | 4 | 4 | 4 | 4 | 4 |
| 16 | 28/09/2016 20:15:05 | A1 | Wilma | 4 | 4 | 4 | 4 | 4 |

Here's the formula I've added in cell A2:

```
=query(Questionnaire!A1:N,"select A, B, C, D, E, F, G, H where A >= date '2016-09-01'
and A <= date '2016-09-30'")
```

The new part is at the end. First, we tell it to look in column A for a date bigger than or equal to the date in inverted commas. Make sure you add the word *date*, to tell the function that you're looking for a date and not some text.

```
where A >= date '2016-09-01'
```

Then in the next part, we add '*and*' to tell it to look for 2 criteria. Then tell it to look for a date less than or equal to the date in inverted commas.

```
and A <= date '2016-09-30'")
```

Note that with dates you need to write the date in the following format:

YYYY-MM-DD

Even if the date format in your sheet is different as it is in my one.

So, to summarise, it gets columns A to H, and returns rows that meet the 2 criteria, i.e. 1/9/2016 to 30/9/2016.

**Example 3b - Filter between 2 dates using cell references**

As we saw earlier, we can replace the actual dates in the formula with cell references.

|   | A | B | C | D | E | F | G | H |
|---|---|---|---|---|---|---|---|---|
| 1 |   | Teacher: | Fred | Start date: | 01/09/2016 | Finish date: | 30/09/2016 |   |
| 2 | timestamp | Level | Teacher's name | Is clear | Is organized | Caters to my needs | Corrects my mistakes | Is punctual |
| 3 | 27/09/2016 09:59:11 | B2 | Betty | 5 | 5 | 5 | 5 | 5 |
| 4 | 27/09/2016 10:07:01 | C1 | Fred | 5 | 5 | 5 | 4 | 5 |
| 5 | 27/09/2016 10:11:39 | B2 | Barney | 5 | 5 | 5 | 5 | 5 |
| 6 | 28/09/2016 10:17:13 | B1 | Wilma | 4 | 3 | 3 | 3 | 2 |
| 7 | 28/09/2016 10:26:21 | B1 | Fred | 4 | 3 | 4 | 3 | 3 |
| 8 | 28/09/2016 11:48:14 | A2 | Barney | 3 | 3 | 4 | 1 | 1 |
| 9 | 28/09/2016 11:55:57 | A1 | Fred | 4 | 3 | 3 | 3 | 3 |
| 10 | 28/09/2016 12:09:47 | A2 | Barney | 5 | 5 | 5 | 5 | 5 |
| 11 | 28/09/2016 12:19:02 | A2 | Betty | 5 | 5 | 5 | 5 | 5 |
| 12 | 28/09/2016 13:43:19 | B1 | Barney | 5 | 5 | 5 | 5 | 4 |
| 13 | 28/09/2016 13:44:29 | B2 | Fred | 4 | 4 | 4 | 4 | 4 |
| 14 | 28/09/2016 13:44:54 | B1 | Wilma | 5 | 5 | 5 | 5 | 5 |
| 15 | 28/09/2016 15:41:47 | B1 | Barney | 4 | 4 | 4 | 4 | 4 |
| 16 | 28/09/2016 20:15:05 | A1 | Wilma | 4 | 4 | 4 | 4 | 4 |

The only thing is that to do this we need quite a complex looking formula. Here's the formula I've added in cell A2:

```
=query(Questionnaire!A1:N,"select A, B, C, D, E, F, G, H where A >= date """&text(D1,"yyyy-MM-dd")&"""
and A <= date """&text(F1,"yyyy-MM-dd")&"""")
```

Here's the formula broken down into its component parts:

```
"select A, B, C, D, E, F, G, H
```

```
where A >= date """&text(D1,"yyyy-MM-dd")&"""

and A <= date """&text(F1,"yyyy-MM-dd")&"""")
```

To replace the actual date, we need to use the following formula after the word 'date':

```
"""&text(D1,"yyyy-MM-dd")&"""
```

This gets the date in cell D1, puts it into the correct format. The same goes for the second date:

```
"""&text(F1,"yyyy-MM-dd")&"""
```

Note, the TEXT function is the same one we used back in chapter 4.

**Example 3c - Filter between 2 dates and by teacher**

Finally, the head wants to filter the feedback between the two dates, by a specific teacher, and order the feedback by date in descending order, as you can see below:

|   | A | B | C | D | E | F | G | H |
|---|---|---|---|---|---|---|---|---|
| 1 |   | Teacher: | Fred | Start date: | 01/09/2016 | Finish date: | 30/09/2016 |   |
| 2 | timestamp | Level | Teacher's name | Is clear | Is organized | Caters to my needs | Corrects my mistakes | Is punctual |
| 3 | 28/09/2016 13:44:29 | B2 | Fred | 4 | 4 | 4 | 4 | 4 |
| 4 | 28/09/2016 11:55:57 | A1 | Fred | 4 | 3 | 3 | 3 | 3 |
| 5 | 28/09/2016 10:26:21 | B1 | Fred | 4 | 3 | 4 | 3 | 3 |
| 6 | 27/09/2016 10:07:01 | C1 | Fred | 5 | 5 | 5 | 4 | 5 |

As you can see the formula is getting pretty long, but you can also see that it's made up of parts and you can extract what you want by adding extra parts.

```
=query(Questionnaire!A1:N,"select A, B, C, D, E, F, G, H where A >= date """&text(D1,"yyyy-MM-dd")&"""
and A <= date """&text(F1,"yyyy-MM-dd")&""" and C='"&B1&"' order by A desc")
```

Here's the query part broken down:

```
"select A, B, C, D, E, F, G, H
```

It gets columns A to H.

```
and A <= date """&text(F1,"yyyy-MM-dd")&"""
```

Finds rows where the date is greater than or equal to the one in cell D1.

```
where A >= date """&text(D1,"yyyy-MM-dd")&"""
```

And that also is less than or equal to the one in cell F1.

```
and A <= date """&text(F1,"yyyy-MM-dd")&"""
```

AND where the name in column C is the same as the name in cell B1.

```
and C='"&B1&"'
```

Then order the results by the dates in column A in descending order.

```
order by A desc")
```

### Example 4 - Filter against various criteria

Here the admin manager wants to use the questionnaire feedback to see how good the information is that is given to the students when they sign up and how well the service was in the office. He particularly wants to know if there was any low feedback in any of the areas under his control, so wants to know if the course info, payment info, or office service was rated less than 3 by anyone.

|   | A | B | C | D | E |
|---|---|---|---|---|---|
| 1 | timestamp | Course information | Payment information | The service in the office was ... | Level |
| 2 | 08/07/2016 16:08:36 | 2 | 4 | 5 | B1 |
| 3 | 13/07/2016 20:03:35 | 2 | 4 | 4 | B1 |
| 4 | 29/08/2016 11:20:10 | 2 | 5 | 4 | B1 |
| 5 | 29/08/2016 11:28:47 | 5 | 5 | 2 | C1 |

To create the table above I've added the following formula in cell A1:

```
=query(Questionnaire!A1:N,"select A, L, M, N, B where L<3 or M<3 or N<3")
```

Here I've selected 5 columns and notice that I've put column B at the end. This shows that when selecting the columns, you don't have to have them in the same order as the original data. This is extremely useful at times.

In the second part, I set the criteria, i.e. he's looking for values which are less than 3 in each of the columns, L, M, and N. To include 3 different criteria, I've used the 'or' keyword, so that it will return rows if any one of them have a value of less than 3 in it.

As we can see in the table above, it's found 3 results where the course information was rated poorly, and we can see from the level that it was related to level B1, so clearly some work is need there.

Plus, there is one incident where the service in the office was rated poorly, which may need investigating.

**Example 5a - Returning the averages of data**

The director of the school wants to know if there are any classrooms that are rated more poorly than others. He wants to see if the average rating is different for any of the classrooms. In the table below, we can see that clearly, there is a problem with class A1, as it is rated poorly and much lower than the others.

|   | A | B |
|---|---|---|
| 1 | Classroom | avg Comfort |
| 2 | | |
| 3 | A1 | 1.9 |
| 4 | A2 | 3.8 |
| 5 | A3 | 3.8 |
| 6 | A4 | 3.4 |
| 7 | A5 | 3.8 |

To do this, I've added the following formula in cell A1:

`=query(Questionnaire!A1:N,"select I, avg(J) group by I")`

This time I'm interested in the classrooms in column I and the average of the scores given in column J. First, I select column I, then select the average of column J, then I group them by classroom, in other words by column I.

We can return the average, count the number of entries, return a maximum or minimum in that column, or sum up the entries, using the following syntax:

| Name | Description | Supported Column Types | Return Type |
|---|---|---|---|
| avg() | Returns the average value of all values in the column for a group. | Number | Number |
| count() | Returns the count of elements in the specified column for a group. Null cells are not counted. | Any type | Number |
| max() | Returns the maximum value in the column for a group. Dates are compared with earlier being smaller, strings are compared alphabetically, with case-sensitivity. | Any type | Same type as column |
| min() | Returns the minimum value in the column for a group. Dates are compared with earlier being smaller, strings are compared alphabetically, with case-sensitivity | Any type | Same type as column |
| sum() | Returns the sum of all values in the column for a group. | Number | Number |

Quite often these work with the *'group by'* keyword, to be able to return the results.

Note, there is an empty row in row 2, as the data range is looking below the original data and into empty rows, and it will return one. This can be eliminated by stating the exact range of your data as we will see next, but the downside is that if more data is added the range will have to be updated.

**Example 5b - Returning the averages of data and ordering them**

Following on from the example above, we can adjust our returned information by sorting the feedback by the lowest to the highest, i.e. in ascending order. Here we can see class A1 is the lowest rated.

|   | A | B |
|---|---|---|
| 1 | Classroom | avg Comfort |
| 2 | A1 | 1.9 |
| 3 | A4 | 3.4 |
| 4 | A3 | 3.8 |
| 5 | A5 | 3.8 |
| 6 | A2 | 3.8 |

Here's the formula I wrote in cell A1:

```
=query(Questionnaire!A1:N44,"select I, avg(J) group by I order by avg(J) asc")
```

The first part is as before, then its follow by:

```
order by avg(J) asc")
```

This orders the results by the average of column J (in column B) in ascending order.

**Example 6 - Pivot information using QUERY not pivot tables**

To finish off this first part, let's look how we can pivot the information to see the averages of 2 criteria for each teacher. We want to look at the "is clear" and "is organised" categories. If you're familiar with pivot tables, this works in a similar way, but with the bonus of doing everything right within the QUERY function.

Here the data has extracted the information below. It looks like Fred's class organisation may need improving a little.

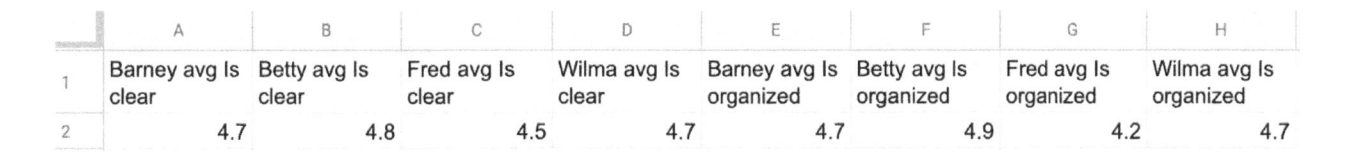

| | A | B | C | D | E | F | G | H |
|---|---|---|---|---|---|---|---|---|
| 1 | Barney avg Is clear | Betty avg Is clear | Fred avg Is clear | Wilma avg Is clear | Barney avg Is organized | Betty avg Is organized | Fred avg Is organized | Wilma avg Is organized |
| 2 | 4.7 | 4.8 | 4.5 | 4.7 | 4.7 | 4.9 | 4.2 | 4.7 |

To get this output, I've written the following formula in cell A1:

```
=query(Questionnaire!A1:N44,"select avg(D), avg(E) pivot C")
```

This selects the average of column D ("is clear") and the average of column E ("is organised") as the criteria, then pivots it by teacher (column C), so that we see an average of each criterion for each teacher.

We could look at every criterion per teacher, just by adding the average for each criteria column, e.g. avg(F), avg(G), etc.

**Analysing a HR database**

OK let's look at a different set of data now. Here we have employee database with some information about them.

|   | A | B | C | D | E |
|---|---|---|---|---|---|
| 1 | **HR Database** | | | | |
| 2 | **Employee** | **Department** | **Salary** | **Years at company** | **Annual bonus** |
| 3 | Fred | Engineering | 30,000€ | 8 | 500€ |
| 4 | Wilma | Engineering | 32,000€ | 12 | 800€ |
| 5 | Betty | Sales | 25,000€ | 8 | 2,000€ |
| 6 | Barney | Admin | 20,000€ | 4 | 1,000€ |
| 7 | John | Sales | 26,000€ | 7 | 2,000€ |
| 8 | Paul | Sales | 28,000€ | 2 | 500€ |
| 9 | George | Admin | 15,000€ | 1 | 200€ |
| 10 | Ringo | Admin | 18,000€ | 3 | 200€ |
| 11 | Baz | Engineering | 31,000€ | 10 | 2,500€ |
| 12 | Mercedes | Sales | 26,000€ | 10 | 2,000€ |

**Example 7 - Returning average salaries per department**

The HR director wants to know what the average salary is per department from the data above. Here's the end result:

|   | A | B |
|---|---|---|
| 1 | Department | avg Salary |
| 2 | Admin | 17,667€ |
| 3 | Engineering | 31,000€ |
| 4 | Sales | 26,250€ |

In cell A1, I've written the following formula:

```
=query(HR!A2:E12,"select B, avg(C) group by B")
```

This selects the departments (column B), and the average of the salaries (column C) grouped by department.

**Example 8 - Listing salaries per employee in descending order**

Here he wants to see the salaries per person in descending order, without any of the other information.

|   | A | B |
|---|---|---|
| 1 | Employee | Salary |
| 2 | Wilma | 32,000€ |
| 3 | Baz | 31,000€ |
| 4 | Fred | 30,000€ |
| 5 | Paul | 28,000€ |
| 6 | John | 26,000€ |
| 7 | Mercedes | 26,000€ |
| 8 | Betty | 25,000€ |
| 9 | Barney | 20,000€ |
| 10 | Ringo | 18,000€ |
| 11 | George | 15,000€ |

In cell A1, I've written the following formula:

`=query(HR!A2:E12,"select A, C order by C desc")`

This selects columns A and C, and sorts column C in descending order.

## Example 9 - Limiting the number of results

The HR director actually only wants to see the 5 highest salaries. We can use the formula and add a limit to it, to show the following:

|   | A | B |
|---|---|---|
| 1 | Employee | Salary |
| 2 | Wilma | 32,000€ |
| 3 | Baz | 31,000€ |
| 4 | Fred | 30,000€ |
| 5 | Paul | 28,000€ |
| 6 | John | 26,000€ |

Here's the formula:

`=query(HR!A2:E12,"select A, C order by C desc limit 5")`

In the last part, I've added 'limit 5'. This returns the first 5 rows.

**Example 10 - Ordering by more than 1 criteria**

Let's now look at how we can order our results by 2 or more criteria. Here the HR guy wants to see the employee names, their departments and salaries. He wants the data organised by department then by salary, with the salaries going from highest to lowest.

|   | A | B | C |
|---|---|---|---|
| 1 | Employee | Department | Salary |
| 2 | Barney | Admin | 20,000€ |
| 3 | Ringo | Admin | 18,000€ |
| 4 | George | Admin | 15,000€ |
| 5 | Wilma | Engineering | 32,000€ |
| 6 | Baz | Engineering | 31,000€ |
| 7 | Fred | Engineering | 30,000€ |
| 8 | Paul | Sales | 28,000€ |
| 9 | John | Sales | 26,000€ |
| 10 | Mercedes | Sales | 26,000€ |
| 11 | Betty | Sales | 25,000€ |

To do this, I've written the following formula:

```
=query(HR!A2:E12,"select A, B, C order by B, C desc")
```

This selects columns A, B, and C (employee, department, and salary), orders first by department (B), then by salary (C). Note the syntax, after 'order by' you just add the first column letter, then the second one after a comma.

**Example 11 - Relabelling column headers**

Finally, let's look at how we can rename the column headers to something different from the original data. This can be useful, if the original data is from a computer output and the column headers aren't in everyday English, or you may simply want to change them.

Here I've changed the column "Employee" to "Name" using the QUERY function.

|   | A | B | C |
|---|---|---|---|
| 1 | Name | Department | Salary |
| 2 | Barney | Admin | 20,000€ |
| 3 | Ringo | Admin | 18,000€ |
| 4 | George | Admin | 15,000€ |
| 5 | Wilma | Engineering | 32,000€ |
| 6 | Baz | Engineering | 31,000€ |
| 7 | Fred | Engineering | 30,000€ |
| 8 | Paul | Sales | 28,000€ |
| 9 | John | Sales | 26,000€ |
| 10 | Mercedes | Sales | 26,000€ |
| 11 | Betty | Sales | 25,000€ |

To do this, yes, you've guessed it, I've added the following formula in cell A1:

`=query(HR!A2:E12,"select A, B, C order by B, C desc label A 'Name'")`

The new part is at the end, (label A 'Name'). This tells it to rename column A with the word 'Name'. To add more labels, just add a comma and the column letter and new name.

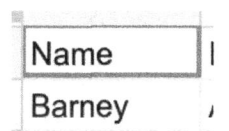

| Name |
|---|
| Barney |

A couple of final comments about QUERY. Be careful where you place your QUERY function, as you need to make sure that there is nothing in the cells particularly below It, as otherwise it'll throw an error.

The syntax is very exact, so make sure you notice in the examples, how the punctuation is used.

Despite this being a long chapter, I've only scratched the surface as to what QUERY is capable of. To learn more, go to Google's page on the query language:

https://developers.google.com/chart/interactive/docs/querylanguage

# A note from the author

I hope you have found this book useful and that you now feel confident in using these functions. There are hundreds of functions and here I've covered the most popular and what I believe the most useful. You can find more information about the functions on the Google spreadsheets function list page here: *https://support.google.com/docs/table/25273?hl=en-GB&ref_topic=1361471*

There are 11 main function categories:
Array, Database, Date, Filter, Google-specific ones, Info, Logical, Lookup, Math, Statistical, and Text. As you can see, they cover all sorts of ways to look at and analyse your data.

The above link contains some good information and is certainly a good starting point but I've found that quite often it doesn't explain them well enough and I've had to go off and look for further information either on people's blogs or on YouTube. This was part of the reason I wrote the material for this book. I felt that there was a lack of material that was detailed enough to help people use these functions well.

In this book, I have assumed you know the basics of using a spreadsheet, for example, entering data in the cells and some basic formatting but if you don't, I would recommend reading my book/ebook *"Beginner's Guide to Google Sheet"*.

If you have any questions about the content of this book, then please contact me at baz@bazroberts.com

**FEEDBACK**
I would love to hear your thoughts on this book! It would be great, if you could spare a minute to fill in this short feedback form:

bit.ly/BazsBooks

Thank you!
Barrie "Baz" Roberts

Rev13

Books and ebooks available by this author on Amazon:

| Beginner's Guide to Google Drive | Beginner's Guide to Google Sheets | Beginner's Guide to Google Docs | Google Sheet Functions – A step-by-step guide |
|---|---|---|---|
|  |  |  |  |
| Step-by-step guide to Google Forms | Step-by-step guide to Google Sites | Step-by-step guide to Google Slides | Step-by-step guide to Google Meet |
|  |  |  |  |

Want to take your Google Sheet skills even further? Learn **Google Apps Script** to be able to automate Google Sheets, Forms, etc. No coding knowledge needed.

| Beginner's Guide to Google Apps Script 1 – Sheets | <ul><li>This book takes you through the first steps of using Apps Script with Google Sheets to automate tasks and go beyond using functions.</li><li>It goes through the basics of JavaScript and Apps Script.</li><li>It then goes through the SpreadsheetApp and the main classes: Spreadsheet, Sheet, and Range – teaching you along the way how to work with Google Sheets.</li><li>Filled with dozens of practical examples of how to use Apps Script with Google Sheets.</li><li>Once you start, you'll never look back!</li></ul> |
|---|---|

| Beginner's Guide to Google Apps Script 2 – Forms  | <ul><li>Learn how to automate **Google Forms** with Apps Script. It covers:<ul><li>Creating and updating Google Forms</li><li>Adding different types of questions to a form</li><li>Using form responses</li><li>Adding form validation</li><li>Adding page navigation – making a clocking in & out form</li><li>Making quizzes in Forms</li></ul></li></ul> |
|---|---|
| Beginner's Guide to Google Apps Script 3 – Drive  | <ul><li>This book goes through using Apps Script with **Google Drive**. It covers:</li><li>Creating files and folders in My Drive and in a specific folder</li><li>Making copies of files</li><li>Creating folders from a URL</li><li>Moving files and folders and adding shortcuts</li><li>Adding and removing editors</li><li>Copying a Google Doc and making a PDF from it</li><li>Getting contents of a Drive folder</li><li>Getting files by type</li><li>Creating download URLs</li><li>Automatically send a brochure when a Form is submitted</li><li>Searching for files and folders</li></ul> |
| Step-by-step Guide to Google Apps Script 4 – Documents  | <ul><li>This book goes through using Apps Script with **Google Docs.** It covers:</li><li>Creating a Google Doc from a form submission</li><li>Master Document copier</li><li>Edit a document template using placeholders</li><li>Making an invoice with multiple items</li><li>Making a document from scratch</li><li>Making student reports with progress bars</li><li>Emailing reports as a PDF or as a link</li><li>Creating multiple reports in one document</li><li>Emailing specific conference information</li></ul> |

|  | • Sending conference info via a web app |
|  | • Update document from data on the web |

| Google Apps Script Projects 1 | • This book goes through 8 real-world practical projects step-by-step to help you practise your Apps Script skills. Projects: |
|  | • Book inventory |
|  | • Make sheets and documents per student |
|  | • Placement test |
|  | • Copy folder content |
|  | • Set up new employee |
|  | • Issues reporting with translation |
|  | • Multiple files and folder maker |
|  | • Send certificates to students |

| Google Apps Script Projects 2 | • This book goes through 8 real-world practical projects step-by-step to help you practise your Apps Script skills. Projects: |
|  | • Mail merge using draft emails |
|  | • Make multiple short URL links for pre-filled Google Forms |
|  | • Date maker taking holidays into account |
|  | • Send emails: 6 easy-to-use templates |
|  | • Creating Calendar events and Meet links |
|  | • Online exam maker |
|  | • Extracting data from Excel |
|  | • Book Inventory: Web app |

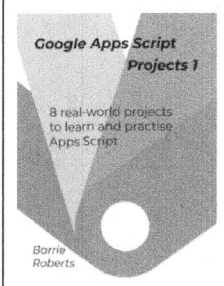

| | |
|---|---|
| JavaScript Fundamentals for Apps Script Users | • This book is aimed at those who are learning Google Apps Script and also want to learn the key concepts of JavaScript.<br>• In this book all explanations and examples are in the context of using JavaScript with Apps Script.<br>• It includes free access to a file containing all the code explained in the book.<br>• Every chapter contains clear explanations and examples focussing more on the use of it rather than the terminology.<br>• It also includes examples using the latest versions of JavaScript. |

I also post and share articles, news and information related to Google Workspace and Apps Script on my website www.bazroberts.com and on social media:

Twitter: twitter.com/barrielroberts

Medium: medium.com/@bazroberts

LinkedIn: https://www.linkedin.com/in/bazroberts/

Facebook: www.facebook.com/bazrobertsgoogleworkspace Search for @bazrobertsgoogleworkspace

Instagram: www.instagram.com/bazroberts_googleworkspace/

Flipboard: flipboard.com/@barrieroberts

# Index

Below is an index of all 66 functions that appear in this book:

- AND: 50–51, 53
- ARRAYFORMULA: 42–43, 88
- AVERAGE: 8–9, 62, 127, 128
- CHAR: 30
- CHOOSE: 118
- CONCATENATE: 26–30, 40
- COUNT: 11, 15, 72, 130
- COUNTA: 12, 15
- COUNTIF: 54–58, 62
- COUNTIFS: 62
- COUNTUNIQUE: 108
- DAY: 114
- DETECTLANGUAGE: 123–124
- EDATE: 121
- EOMONTH: 121–122
- FILTER: 66–74
- FIND: 89–90
- GOOGLETRANSLATE: 123–126
- HOUR: 116
- HYPERLINK: 138–141
- IF: 17–25, 48–52, 97
- IFERROR: 36, 125
- IMAGE: 134–135
- IMPORTRANGE: 75–84
- INDEX: 142–146
- ISEMAIL: 94, 97, 101–102
- ISNUMBER: 95, 97, 103
- ISURL: 96–97, 103
- LEFT: 88–89
- LEN: 88–89
- LOWER: 86, 88–89
- MATCH: 142–146
- MAX: 9
- MID: 89–90
- MIN: 10
- MINUTE: 116
- MONTH: 71, 115–116
- NETWORKDAYS: 119–120, 122
- NETWORKDAYS.INTL: 122
- NOT: 102–103
- NOW: 111
- OFFSET: 127–131
- OR: 48, 52
- PROPER: 85, 87–88
- QUERY: 147–161
- RIGHT: 88–89
- ROUND: 137
- ROUNDDOWN: 137
- ROUNDUP: 137

- SECOND: 116
- SORT: 105, 109–110
- SUBSTITUTE: 89–90
- SUM: 7, 15, 29, 38, 73, 130
- SUMIF: 59, 115
- SUMIFS: 60
- TEXT: 30, 152, 153
- TODAY: 69, 112, 113, 115, 116
- TRANSPOSE: 91–93
- TRIM: 87
- UNIQUE: 104–105, 109, 110
- UPPER: 86, 88, 89
- VLOOKUP: 33–47, 143–145
- WEEKDAY: 52–53, 117–118
- WORKDAY: 118–119
- WORKDAY.INTL: 122
- YEAR: 115–116

Made in the USA
Middletown, DE
01 February 2023